# KOPS AND CUSTARDS
*The Legend of Keystone Films*

I have often thought that the funniest gag in the world could be made out of the coronation of a king—if it were not for the expense.

I can imagine how the king would be coming down the street on the way to be crowned, with the life guards and the brass bands and the carriages, with outriders and all. But when he gets to the palace where the coronation is to take place, he can't get in. The janitor comes out and searches frantically for the door key. Can't find it. His wife has been pressing his pants with the family flatiron and forgot to put the key back into his pocket. So the king and all the royalty have to wait until the janitor hot-foots it home to ask the wife what she did with the stuff in his pockets when she ironed his pants.

That's the very essence of comedy. That's the stuff it is made of— contrast and catastrophe involving the unseating of dignity.

MACK SENNETT

# KOPS AND CUSTARDS
## The Legend of Keystone Films

## (A BOOK)

### By Kalton C. Lahue
### and Terry Brewer

WITH A FOREWORD BY
KENT D. EASTIN

UNIVERSITY OF OKLAHOMA PRESS : NORMAN

BY KALTON C. LAHUE

*Continued Next Week: A History of the Moving Picture Serial*
(Norman, 1964)
*World of Laughter: The Motion Picture Comedy Short, 1910–1930*
(Norman, 1966)

BY KALTON C. LAHUE AND TERRY BREWER
*Kops and Custards: The Legend of Keystone Films* (Norman, 1968)

LIBRARY OF CONGRESS CATALOG CARD NUMBER: 67–24625

*For Frank Leon Smith—and the American Dream*

# Foreword

By Kent D. Eastin

For anyone whose movie-going experiences began in the second decade of this century or earlier, there were highlights among the silents that evoke warm memories. The possibility is great that one of the fondest of these recollections is of Mack Sennett's Keystone Comedies, for these films offered something fresh and spontaneous, unfettered and uninhibited, and they moved across the screen at a pace which the movies, up until then, had not otherwise achieved. Appearing in the Keystone Comedies were personalities that had a certain spark—ignited by Sennett—not usually in evidence in the more pedantic "comedy" offerings of other producers of the period.

My own "going-to-the-movies" began about the time of World War I. I had just missed the Keystone period and have no recollection of ever having seen an authentic Keystone Comedy at the time of its original release. I do remember seeing a few of the Keystone-Chaplins in their reissue by W. H. Productions and some of the other Keystones during their frequent reappearances well into the middle 1920's.

By 1918 and 1919, Sennett had real competition, even though his productions—no longer Keystones—were distributed by Paramount, at that time the top company in the business. While Sennett's comedies were then more elaborate in character, fewer of them were being produced than in the heyday of Keystone. For some unknown reason, I did not see a great many of the Sennett comedies during those two years, nor during 1920 and 1921 when they were distributed by United Artists and First National. My favorites of the day were the "Lonesome Luke" comedies with Harold Lloyd, produced by Hal Roach and distributed by Pathé; the Fatty Arbuckle comedies, produced by Joseph M. Schenck, which were distributed by Paramount; and the stunt comedies of Larry Semon, produced and distributed by Vitagraph. But there were hundreds of other comedies made every year, and when some routine offering of the time had something less than the whole-hearted approval of the audience, I remember overhearing comments that ran something like this: "It wasn't as good as the Key-stones used to be!"

It was memories such as this on which the Keystone legend is based.

To the public at large today, the name Keystone in connection with the movies probably means the Keystone Cops and their paddy-wagons, custard pies, racing trains and automobiles, motor-cycles and airplanes, bathing beauties, and explosions with results ridiculous. But the specifics are pretty vague.

The period in which the Keystone Comedies were produced—1912 to 1917—is far from being the best-documented era of the silent days. Historically it is already a fuzzy age about which many facts are not readily available and in which fact and fiction are so often intermixed that a work such as *Kops and Custards* is not only a needed but most welcome and readable addition to the liter-ature of the motion picture. The authors' research has unearthed much that has been forgotten about Sennett and his Keystone Comedy factory—his stable of clowns and the people who, under his guidance, directed and edited these funny films.

When this five-year period began, the comedies that had reached the screen, other than some of those in which Sennett had a hand at Biograph, were almost completely influenced by the stage. There was no true motion picture comedy form, precedent, or technique. It was a clear field, and what Sennett did with it in that span of five years is what gave the Keystones their impact on the movies of the day and on motion picture comedy for all time to come.

The Keystone influence on the industry was immediate. Players, writers, and directors with a year or two of experience and training with Sennett were attracted to other companies and, to various degrees, carried the Keystone influence with them. From that time on, during the years of the silents, there was hardly a comedy producer of consequence without some Keystone "alumni" under contract.

Sennett's output in the Keystone days was prolific. Literally hundreds of comedies carrying the Keystone name reached the theaters in that five-year period. And while the original negatives of most of them are gone, a surprising number are available for screening today. Contributing to this are three unrelated circumstances.

During the late teens and early twenties, the frequent reissuings of many of the Keystones—some of them again and again—were through states' rights channels, where distribution rights would be sold for a particular territory and for a definite period of time. After paying the agreed-on sum for its territorial license, the exchange would simply purchase the number of prints of each title required for its territory. Most of these distributors were relatively small operators, and when their licenses expired, the prints which they had purchased would be sold to traveling exhibitors, medicine shows, and dealers specializing in the sale of used prints. Down the years, having found their way into the hands of individuals, these old 35mm. prints are turning up in some barn, shed, or long-closed small-town opera house where someone's father or grandfather had left them long ago.

Somewhat similar to this pattern of 35mm. theatrical release was the distribution of a number of the Keystones, principally from the Triangle period, on 28mm. film—the nontheatrical standard of those primitive days—through Pathéscope Libraries. A modest selection of Keystones were licensed to Pathéscope on a basis whereby 28mm. prints were both rented and sold. This placed prints in the hands of many individuals. And, being made on the early "non-inflammable" stock which was not subject to the same decomposition hazards as the usual inflammable film, many of these 28mm. prints have survived in relatively excellent condition and adapt today to quite successful conversion to 16mm. and 8mm. Further, during part of the years 1914 and 1915, two 35mm. paper prints each of almost one hundred of the Keystone Comedies were deposited with the Copyright Office of the Library of Congress in Washington in connection with the copyright of the subjects. This practice, required before mid-1912 because the only way a producer of a motion picture could get copyright protection was to copyright the film as a photograph, was no longer essential or even pertinent. Why it was done by Keystone at that time is not known.

Most of the Keystone Comedies were not copyrighted, and of those that were, I know of none on which the copyright was renewed during the twenty-eighth year of the original copyright period, as required to extend the copyright to the full fifty-six years. Because of this, practically all of the Keystones today are in the public domain and may be freely converted to 16mm. and 8mm. More and more are thus becoming available every year for purchase or rental, and even on a free loan basis from many public libraries.

It is from these and other sources that Kalton Lahue and Terry Brewer have been able to determine who directed and who appeared in so many of the Keystones. More than that, it is their hunting out countless trade publications, press releases, early fan magazines, production company brochures, records, and scripts, and the locating and interviewing of many of the persons who were connected with Keystone, that has enabled them to so thoroughly reconstruct the titles of these hundreds of comedies that made up the whole spread of Keystone production, filling it in to such a substantial degree with the name of the players who appeared in most of the films and the directors of many.

For those of us who have a fair present-day knowledge of the Keystones that are available, it gives an added dimension to the story. And to those who know the Keystones only from the film clips frequently seen on television—hardly more than previews in the modern sense—*Kops and Custards* is a review of the whole span of those funny, flickery, and fabulous years when the things Mack Sennett accomplished made him the undisputed father of silent screen comedy.

Come along—turn back the pages of time—join the chase! You can be part of it in *Kops and Custards!*

# Introduction

THIS VOLUME is an attempt to give an inside view of the Keystone Film Company and how it grew. Although nothing like it has been written in the English language up to this time, no claim is made for this as a definitive work on the subject. Any such claim would be sheer foolishness, for the entire and complete truth cannot be objectively fashioned until the crates of documents which Sennett donated to the Academy of Motion Picture Arts and Sciences have been opened, catalogued, studied, and evaluated.

Why, then, write this particular book now? The answer is a simple and—we hope—a reasonable one. The Sennett collection has been untouched since it was donated over a decade ago. At the present time, the Academy merely serves as a storehouse for this mass of raw history. A lack of funds and interest on the part of those who could support such research will probably prevent any serious study for another two or three decades. Such neglect is eloquent testimony to the shameful status of motion-picture history.

But while film scholars are waiting for the Academy to make the Sennett collection available for study, there is no guarantee that it will escape the ravages of time. Fire or water could possibly cause untold damage, further delaying examination of the vast quantity of information. What follows should be regarded as an interim report, serving to correct errors of the past while awaiting the volume which the Sennett collection will hopefully provide some fortunate film historian many years from now.

In researching this work, primary sources such as trade papers, production reports, scripts, and letters were used, supplemented where possible by the files and memories of private parties. The Academy of Motion Picture Arts and Sciences provided much information and assistance, as did the California State Library in Sacramento and the Adam Kessel estate. The Mountain View Public Library arranged many interlibrary loans of valuable and rare material.

Chester Conklin, Minta Durfee, Tom Kennedy, Eddie Gribbon, and Dot Farley provided general information about Keystone and Sennett, while Mrs. William Horsley was responsible for many insights into Sennett's personality. William Campbell's recollections regarding the writing and directing staffs and their functions, as well as Fred Balshofer's knowledge of the early days of Keystone and the behind-the-scenes intrigues proved very useful. Kent D. Eastin's deep interest in the world of silent movies is exceeded only by his willingness to encourage when spirits are low and to loan materials when they are needed.

Many other persons too numerous to give individual mention graciously furnished films and other materials from their private collections. Secondary sources are listed in the bibliography for the reader who wishes to explore further the myths, legends, and half-truths concerning Keystone and its founders.

KALTON C. LAHUE
TERRY BREWER

# Contents

# Illustrations

Kops and Custards

KOPS AND CUSTARDS
*The Legend of Keystone Films*

# *Prologue*

IT HAS BECOME quite fashionable over the years, when discussing motion pictures and comedy, to regard the name Mack Sennett with a large degree of awe and respect. His name is synonymous with the designation "King of Comedy" and has taken on the aura of a legend. Created early in his career, the legend had been in existence for many years before he retired from actively producing comedies.

A legend always has some basis in fact, but as the story is handed from one to another, fiction becomes a junior partner with fact. Soon the two tend to merge, and truth is transformed into legend. Legend also requires a fascinating character whose accomplishments and exploits increase as time passes. Sennett's colorful personality and his achievements met this requirement.

Even today, years after Sennett departed from this life, the legend continues to grow and thrive. He had no apparent peer in the realm of silent-screen comedy. His closest competitor, Hal Roach, is still alive, but no such adulation has grown up around his career.[1] Al Christie is virtually forgotten.

It is clear that when a man so far outdistanced his many con-

[1] Hal Roach is becoming recognized today, but mainly because of his association with Stanley Laurel and Oliver Hardy, who have been rediscovered as a classic comedy team whose timeless routines merit serious attention.

temporaries as to foster a living legend, there must have been a reason which brought this about. The reason is contained within another legend, the Keystone Film Company. The name Keystone shares a luster equivalent to the name of Sennett. Whenever the word is used, it conjures up visions of zany comedians, careening cars, Kops, and custards.

From its very beginning, Keystone was considered to be the best of silent slapstick, but today we often forget that it was not really representative of the field of visual comedy. Rather, Keystone stands as a unique example of what could be done with a camera and a group of dedicated men. It is the outgrowth of one man's philosophy of comedy, which happened to tickle the funny bone of a nation. It is ingenuity, native perception, and an innate sense of human follies.

It is also a reflection of the America of an earlier day—an America untroubled by the problems which we face today; an America in which an uneducated former boilermaker and ironworker could rise to the top of his profession and walk side by side with hereditary wealth. The day is long past when this can be accomplished so easily, but the day is not past for the healthy and hearty laughter which Keystone provided for a generation with its own problems to solve.

America was still maturing in the early twentieth century, and there was still a naïve sense of "manifest destiny" that was yet to be fulfilled. Customs and ways of life were in the process of changing into a complex system from which there could be no escape. A youthful nation was on the threshold of a greatness which few realized lay ahead. There was a need then, as there always has been and ever will be, for relief from the burden of daily life. This relief was provided by the new invention: motion pictures. But to a greater extent, it was provided by one segment of the movie world—the comedy.

Screen comedy was lifted from a rather drab existence by one man and one company: Mack Sennett's Keystone. It was reoriented and skillfully packaged in a version which could be appreciated by those people who needed it the most, America's working middle class, who were the people responsible in large measure for America's growth and greatness. These people came from the same stock and the same background as Mack Sennett, and therein lay the great success of the Keystone comedies. They appealed to common men, whom God created far in excess of uncommon men.

The history of the Keystone Film Company that follows is inescapably a history of the youthful Mack Sennett, for its trials and tribulations were his. The company's successes and failures can be placed only at his doorstep, for Sennett exercised as near total control over Keystone as could any man who operated a million-dollar business in those golden days before World War I.

But, as is often the case, the legend of Keystone became greater than the sum of its parts. Those individuals who were responsible for its acceptance were, for the most part, unable to rise above the myth which they had helped to create. Of the comics, only Chaplin found the magic route to a fame equaling that of Keystone. The rest were unable to transfer their talents with any degree of success. This is not to demean them, but only to show that the task was nearly insurmountable. As a group, they had done their work too well; as individuals, they could not surpass it.

# 1. The Luck of the Irish

DURING THE nineteenth century it was not a handicap for any youngster to be born a Catholic in the province of Quebec. But if he happened to be born into an Irish family, the child needed more than a smile from St. Patrick to succeed in that French stronghold of Canada, for the Irish found no more welcome there than they had in Boston. The luck of the Irish is exactly what smothered young Michael Sinnott. Born in Richmond, Province of Quebec,[1] on January 17, 1880, he quickly grew into a gangling lad whose arms (by his own description) nearly touched the floor, even when he stood erect. His father was a farmer, an occupation still common in rural Quebec. For some years John Sinnott also found it necessary to operate a small hotel in the village to support his brood of four.

Michael's early life was not one of luxury, but it was not touched with the desperate poverty which was the lot of many Quebec farmers of the time. Rather, his family lived in a middle-class existence founded upon a cash income of about $1,400 yearly, a rather decent wage for that time. Michael's slight acquaintance with formal education was gained in several schools. The family moved from Richmond (or Denville) to Megantic, which brought about

[1] Or Denville, P.Q., depending upon your source.

one change of schools. Not by any stretch of the imagination was Michael ever considered to be a good student, a fact which helped to acquaint him with many other schools. He failed miserably in an attempt to learn grammar and its proper usage, and this handicap followed him throughout life. Although bilingual, speaking was always a slow and difficult task for the boy. He was equally lost in either French or English.

To add to young Michael's problems, he dreamed of becoming a singer, even after his voice changed when he was fifteen. Irish tenors are universally admired, but an Irish bass? Friends, neighbors, and family tried to discourage the lad's desire to express himself in song. John Sinnott went so far as to caution his son that no good ever came to anyone who insisted on singing bass. Catherine Sinnott did not know music (which was just as well), thus she did not express surprise when Michael confessed that his heart's desire was to sing opera—in Italian. Mothers often blind themselves to their offsprings' failings, and Catherine was no different. She admired her son's ambitions and fostered them whenever it was possible. Looking back now, it was a combination of the boy's determination to sing and his Irish luck that brought Michael along the path to fame and fortune.

When he was seventeen, the Sinnott family moved to the United States. John Sinnott had finally decided that there was little future in trying to earn a living from the rocky Canadian soil. Since Catherine had relatives in Connecticut, the Sinnotts decided to seek a new life there. Handy with carpenter tools, it was easy for John to find a job working for a contractor. Catherine turned her new home into a boarding house, and Michael located work in the American Iron Works. A relative, Peter Comisky, was employed there, and he quickly took Michael under his guidance. The young man stood six foot one and weighed 210 pounds; physically, he was well equipped for the hot, hard life of an ironworker.

The wages were 15 cents an hour and the work week consisted of sixty hours, which gave the lad a total of $9 for his week's labors. He earned every cent of it—carrying iron rails on his shoulder, driving red-hot rivets with a ten-pound sledge hammer, and skimming the slag from pools of molten iron heated to 3,500°. Life in the ironworks was rugged, and the hard work of lifting and hammering brought tempers to the boiling point easily. Michael had his share of brawls with fellow workers. The fact that he insisted on occasionally giving out with a song or two did little to endear him to ears already filled with the loud and harsh sounds around them.

Catherine's boardinghouse earned an average of $70 weekly, but much of this money was spent to feed the boarders. They were also ironworkers, and their appetites matched their physiques. The well-stocked dining table was a shambles by the time each meal was finished. It was here that Michael met his first music teacher, a small man who encouraged the lad's singing. The fee for each lesson was one dinner, accompanied by 50 cents in cash, but in Catherine's eyes this was a small price to pay for such artistry. It was not long before Michael had learned a few songs. Every night after the table had been cleared, he stood in front of a captive audience and sang. The boarders failed to appreciate this entertainment, but good manners kept them from showing their disapproval.

By the time he was eighteen, Michael had become discouraged. He had worked in the iron foundry for nearly a year, and now the family had decided to move to Northampton, Massachusetts. This was the opportunity to make a decision. Should he go on with his life as it was set out before him, or should he try to better himself? There was no sympathy forthcoming from John Sinnott. In his father's eyes, the son had a good future—he could handle almost any form of hard labor. Good workers could always find a steady job—why give it up?

On the other hand, Catherine was more romantic in nature than her husband. The Sinnotts were making a living, and Michael was not really needed at home. Why not let the boy try what he wanted so desperately to do? John was eventually won over to Catherine's side, and when *Lady Slavey* opened in Northampton, Michael had charted his course of action. He decided to meet the star of the show and ask her advice on the best way to begin a stage career.

9

Canadian by birth and a comic actress with a fine reputation, Marie Dressler was not yet thirty. Michael was certain that she could be of help to him, if he could only gain a proper introduction. He discussed the question with his mother, and shortly Catherine came upon a solution. She would obtain a letter of introduction from the family lawyer. Calvin Coolidge was still a long way from the reputation that would make him a leading political figure in the 1920's. But at this time his ever-growing law practice testified to a reputation as a practical man. Coolidge was regarded by the local populace as being a man with a future and a good person to know.

The letter from Coolidge opened the stage door of the Academy Theater, and Michael came face to face with the first real actress he had ever seen. Miss Dressler was kind and courteous but quite pessimistic about Michael's chances of finding fame on the stage. Thinking to discourage the starry-eyed country boy, she emphasized the hard work necessary for a start. When he pointed out that the life of an ironworker was hardly one of ease, Miss Dressler broke out with a laugh. The boy had a point; he might just have the necessary fortitude.

She sat down and quickly penned a letter. Addressing it to Mr. David Belasco, Marie handed the envelope to Michael and told him to take it to New York City. Little did she realize that years later a job offer would come to her from this same young man, every bit as grateful in 1914 as he had been in 1899. Thanking her profusely and promising to prove himself worthy of her help, Michael took his leave.

David Belasco, though not yet fifty, had become a powerful influence in the world of the legitimate stage. On his word the destiny of stars and shows turned; he could make or break a play or a player with no difficulty at all. Now in front of his desk there stood a tall, gangling youth whose untrained hair refused to obey the commands of a comb. The suit did not fit his ill-shaped form, nor were its jacket sleeves long enough. As the red-faced boy stood uneasily in front of the impresario, he shifted a battered straw suitcase from one hand to the other, as if he did not quite know

Fred Mace and Mack Sennett, Keystone's two daffy detectives, caught in a pensive mood while filming an early sleuth comedy.

*Courtesy Tom Dino*

Mabel Normand was the heroine and Mack Sennett was a perfect yokel in *The Rube and the Baron* (1913).

what to do with the empty hand. Now and then, Michael would shove it into his pocket, at the same time shifting his weight from one foot to the other. Clearly, thought Belasco, the lad was nervous, but he did have an introduction from Marie Dressler.

What to do with the young fellow? Sinnott wanted to be an actor, but admitted that his only talent consisted of a song or two and a shuffle which he hesitantly called a dance step. Everyone connected with the theater knew that David Belasco was interested only in acting ability. He was not running an agent's office for would-be vaudeville acts. Yet here stood one such young man, devoid of any talent, asking for help and advice. Belasco's sensitive nature seldom surfaced when he was engaged in business dealings, but there was something about this youth that he liked. Certainly it was not talent; it must have been his naïve determination. Belasco could not bring himself to have the lad removed—that would have been a discourtesy to Miss Dressler—but neither could he offer much encouragement.

Once Michael had fully explained his desire, Belasco could think of only one helpful suggestion: "Go home!" This failed to make any noticeable impression on the young man standing before his desk, and Belasco sighed. Practical man that he was, the theatrical magnate then suggested that burlesque would serve as a fine starting point. Here Michael could learn the rudiments of acting, and in the process he might realize that the stage was not to be his calling after all.

Thanking Belasco for his trouble, Michael went back to his boardinghouse to think things over. Alone in New York City, he had only $25 to his name. He was on the fringe of show business, for his fellow boarders were entertainers—midgets, dancers, singers, and carnival folk. Broadway and its gas lamps fascinated Michael, and he really did not feel a world apart from those men who inhabited the Great White Way (as it would soon be known), even if they did dress in white tie and tails. No, the social distinctions made little impression on the dreaming country boy. Here was the world of show business, and he wanted to be a part of it. Only a job stood between him and his ambitions, and Michael knew that he could find that job. It would be a start, and one day his mother would be proud that her boy had fulfilled a promise. Michael Sinnott would be somebody; he would be a noted personality in the entertainment world. Men and women alike would crowd around him when he entered a restaurant. Dreams, dreams, dreams; would they ever become a reality?

Michael thought so, and thus the Bowery Theater Burlesque soon acquired a new patron. Michael went down daily for at least one performance to size up his future. The "burlycue" of that day was delightful to its patrons. The German dialect comics, the fat dancing girls, and the cop-tramp comedy acts approached life with an earthy sense of understanding. Authority was reduced to an absurdity, pretension was insulted with nonsense, and all of the follies and foibles of humanity came under the comic eye of burlesque. It all added up to great fun for the audiences, even though few could see any meaning other than what took place on the stage. Michael was no different; he could not and did not try to analyze these things. He just found them to be funny and interesting—a world he could understand and enjoy.

Having decided upon his calling, the former ironworker had only to get a job and he would be on his way. Hanging around the Bowery Theater, Michael made a few friends and soon had his position—a character role as the hind part of a horse. This also served to introduce him to more friends—the police. The Bowery Theater was raided, and the entire cast wound up in jail. Michael's explanation of his presence in the show and of his plans for the future gained him his freedom with only an admonition from the judge. He was told to return to the honest labor of the ironworks and lead a respectable life.

This advice was accepted gratefully and ignored easily. Back at work in burlesque and once more earning money, he located another singing tutor who was willing to accept him as a student. Shortly after this, the young Canadian decided that a singing career was not for him. It was not the knowledge or belief that he had too little talent which finally brought about his decision; it was

14

simply a realization that too much time and money had to be expended before success would arrive.

But Michael Sinnott had drive and ambition, characteristics that were firmly rooted in his Irish background. John Sinnott had always encouraged his son to do his best, and even though Michael had embarked on a course which was not heartily approved by his father, the boy was determined to make something of himself. Now, at twenty-two, he was on the threshold of a new era. The twentieth century had arrived, and the pace of life was beginning to accelerate. As he often expressed it, there was no place to go but up.

With his livelihood assured by his employment at the Bowery Theater and by the continued support of his mother in the form of encouraging letters containing cash, Michael became firmly settled in his new world. Looking for advancement, he took to the road with touring companies and played the circuits. He sang in quartets, clowned, and carried scenery for $18 weekly.

This was only a beginning, and Michael refused to regard it in any other way. He had learned that burlesque was a hard way to make a living, and while the other actors were decent and considerate to him, they were a far cry from the tasteful, talented people who dominated the Broadway scene. As soon as Michael returned to New York City, he tried out for a part in Raymond Hitchcock's musical, *King Dodo*. On the strength of his deep voice he landed a role in the chorus, but the dancing requirement proved to be his downfall. His shuffling had been quite acceptable on the circuits, but it hardly sufficed for the big time. Once, after inadvertently tripping the star of the show, Michael was shown to the door. As he left, Michael had a few choice words for Hitchcock. The tables would turn and one day, in the not-too-distant future, Hitchcock would go to work for Michael Sinnott.

*A Chinese Honeymoon*, starring Thomas Seabrooke, found Michael in the chorus with Fred Mace, another man whom he would hire in the future. By this time he had changed his name to Mack Sennett and had acquired a habit which would serve him well throughout life. Questioning the star, or any other person in the show who was willing to co-operate, Mack tried to pick up any form of useful information. While playing in *Wang*, DeWolf Hopper pointed out the value of not giving the audience everything at one time. His advice was always to keep something in reserve, and Mack noted it as a good point to remember. Other shows followed quickly: *Piff! Paff!! Pouff!!!* starring Eddie Foy; *Mlle Modiste* with Fritzi Scheff; and *The Boys of Company B* with young John Barrymore, bringing his career up to the year 1908.

The motion-picture industry was growing out of its infancy at this time. Edwin S. Porter had made *The Great Train Robbery* for Edison in 1903, but the great boom in nickelodeon growth did not occur until about 1906. Edison, Vitagraph, Selig, Lubin, Kalem, and Essanay were expanding daily, as was the Biograph Company. Mack Sennett was twenty-seven years old, soon to be twenty-eight, and he had heard that there was money to be made in the movies.

Sennett was earning a living, but what he really wanted was more than a living. Like most young Americans of the time, he could imagine himself surrounded by wealth—able to buy anything he wanted, able to eat in the finest restaurants and to rub shoulders with the best people. The living which he was earning was just that—a living. If the movies offered money, that was exactly where Mack wanted to be. Other actors might complain that "shadow-acting" was beneath their dignity, but to one who had started his show-business career as the hind end of a horse, money outweighed dignity. And so, he did just what many other enterprising would-be actors had done. Mack applied for a job at 11 East 14th Street, the home of Biograph. As his Irish luck would have it, "Pop" McCutcheon, the studio manager, put him to work on his twenty-eighth birthday, January 17, 1908. The salary was $5 a day.

Biograph was a respected name in the world of "flickers." It had the best actors, directors, and stories. The audiences might not know the names of the players, but the mere mention that a Biograph film was playing in the neighborhood nickelodeon would pack the house. Fans knew what they liked and Biograph tried hard to give it to them, at the same time maintaining an aura of respectability around their product. Sennett had stumbled into the fascinating world of make-believe at a time when the industry was still extremely fluid. A great demand existed for actors, actresses, extras, day workers, writers, and the like. For a young man with imagination, the desire to excel by hard work, and a modicum of talent, the field was wide open. It was here that Mack Sennett, born Michael Sinnott, was to gain an education that would soon be worth millions of dollars to him.

Biograph had on its payroll another young man, the reserved and proud David Griffith. Frustrated actor that he was, Griffith had joined the company in an effort to assure himself a daily meal. He soon began to assert his ideas and Biograph made him a director, with the guarantee of an acting job should he fail to make good. Griffith never returned to acting; instead he rose to a position of prominence as the godfather of the industry, and was regarded as a true cinematic genius. For many years his name was breathed with reverence, and he gloried in the homage paid to him.

Griffith did not realize it at the time, but he was teaching the fundamentals of the motion-picture business to Mack Sennett, who would also become a figure larger than life. Sennett was not constantly busy with his acting chores, so between takes, during lunch and at other odd times during the day, he had ample opportunity to observe Griffith at work. He also discovered that D. W., as Griffith was known, liked to walk. When Griffith walked, Mack fell into step beside him and asked question after question. Busy as he was, Griffith seemed to like the attention and started using Sennett as a sounding board for his ambitions. He discussed what he was trying to do with the screen and what he hoped to do in the near future. His forte was drama—he saw stories as close-ups dramatized by tragedy.

Sennett made certain that he was walking in the same direction as Griffith every night after work, and he began to expound some of his own ideas about the techniques of making pictures. Sennett was anxious to discuss his theories on the possibilities of screen comedy, a topic which left Griffith completely unmoved. Griffith

17

failed to see anything funny about comic policemen, regardless of the manner in which Sennett chose to present his thesis or how many times he explained it. The topic bored Griffith then, just as it would bore him after his walking companion became world famous. Nonetheless, he was tolerant of Sennett's opinions, and as they strolled about the city, the two men discussed motion pictures and the great new future in front of them.

Sennett played extra and walk-on roles between his discussions with Griffith, as well as an occasional leading part. His big chance came with a role in *The Curtain Pole,* a three-quarter-reel comedy of 1909.[2] This film was well received and Sennett became recognized for his ability to smash, wreck, and demolish sets, creating havoc on screen. This part was followed by a role in *The Politician's Love Story,* a picture with police in it. Sennett did not play a policeman; he was cast (much to his dismay) as the lead in a silk hat complete with moustache.

Sennett had ambitions for cops and comedy, and his feelings were no secret. He believed that a policeman, as the symbol of authority and dignity, was a perfect foil for comedy. Burlesque had taught Sennett that deflation of authority was a positive manner in which to get laughs. Preposterous dress made Sennett's policeman more dignified and stuffy, thereby emphasizing his reduction to an absurd symbol. Sennett was certain that he had something in his idea, but who would listen?

Biograph executives were not interested in the idea. Just as Griffith had been, they were more concerned with drama and what they considered to be a respectable product. Comedy as a supplement to drama was considered fine, but pure slapstick for its own sake had no place in their scheme of things. Had Biograph taken a different attitude, it might not have fallen upon evil times when Griffith finally decided to rebel against its rock-ribbed conserva-

---

2 This was his fourth film appearance. Sennett had previously been seen in *Balked at the Altar* (1908), *Father Gets in the Game* (1908), and *Mr. Jones Had a Card Party* (1909). Some film historians regard *The Curtain Pole* as the first genuine farcical slapstick comedy to be made in America.

Films were released in a standard length of one reel, which held one thousand feet of footage. A split reel was one which contained two different subjects of varying lengths to equal one thousand feet.

tive thinking. But regardless of Biograph's many other faults, the company would not turn down scenarios, and this was the next field that Sennett was determined to conquer.

Mary Pickford had joined the organization, and quickly began to supplement her acting income by writing and selling stories to Biograph. She appeared to understand Sennett's dilemma with comedy and even encouraged him to write. Mack's first effort was considered excellent until the front office inadvertently discovered that it bore more than a passing resemblance to an O. Henry story in *The New York World*. Sennett thus discovered that writing scenarios was not as easy as he had thought, and began seriously to study the writers he knew. He discussed their trade with them and began to copy the methods of operation of these knowledgeable souls.

Biograph continued to read his stories, thereby encouraging the frustrated comedian. He soon reached that degree of proficiency which was necessary to sell his stories with some regularity. Of course, his scenarios were not much as screenplays go, but then few were in those days. Most screen stories of the time were nothing more than a number of quick dramatic scenes. One of the most famous scripts done by Sennett was *The Lonely Villa*, an early film with Mary Pickford. Its quality raised his payment to $25 per story, a handsome sum in those days. To Sennett, this was quite the life. He had come a long way since Northampton, but there was still a longer way to go. He knew it and was eager to move on to greater things.

# 2. *Two Race Track Touts*

Motion pictures were growing by leaps and bounds.[1] The growth of nickelodeons continued, but in addition real movie palaces began to appear.[2] At the start of 1909, the daily attendance at picture shows was a staggering 3,000,000 persons. The 1,095,-000,000 annual viewers deposited an estimated $57,500,000 into the hands of exhibitors. A survey of the nine largest cities in the United States showed that there was one theater seat for each 7,622 persons living within the city. By 1911, one person in every 23 attended one of the 13,000 shows presented each day—a nationwide attendance totaling over 4,000,000. Houses devoted to exhibiting motion pictures seated 1,350,000 persons across the country and grossed an estimated $102,000,000 yearly.

Theaters ranged from country storerooms with an investment as little as $500 to city palaces costing $250,000 to $500,000. On a national scale, there was a total investment of $100,000,000 in the business of making and showing movies. The value of films sold in 1910 was $9,000,000 in the United States. Foreign sales raised the figure by an undetermined amount.[3] The demand for film was

[1] Chicago had 300 nickelodeons in 1910; New York City had 450.
[2] For the best description of the growth of movie theaters, see Ben Hall's *The Best Remaining Seats* (Clarkson-Potter, 1961).
[3] *The World's Work* (February, 1911). The figures are given by Asa Steele in his discussion of the industry's growth in the United States.

fantastic, and new producers were moving into the field in increasing numbers. Some made a success of it; most failed and disappeared within a short time.[4]

The magic lantern with its flickering illumination had captured the imagination of a nation, and a huge new industry had been born. For the shrewd man who cared to pioneer in this field, the financial return for his labors was unimaginable. Fabulous times were just around the next corner, and Mack Sennett was right in the thick of things.

Some men were able to foresee the future just a bit, and these were the ones who made fortunes beyond their wildest dreams. They were not college graduates, nor were they theater people in the accepted sense. These men came from varied backgrounds and nearly all were poor. Carl Laemmle (clothing), Adolph Zukor (the fur business), Samuel Goldfish (gloves), Louis B. Mayer and Harry, Sam, and Jack Warner (the junk business) were some of the men destined to forge new lives, fortunes, and immense power for themselves from tiny strips of celluloid. In view of this, it is not surprising that two gamblers could also rise to the top.

Adam Kessel and Charles Bauman had been quite successful in their chosen field, until the reform movement in New York state gained a headway. In 1908, Governor Charles Evans Hughes signed into law a bill which affected their very livelihood. Race track gambling was made illegal in New York. The law was strictly enforced, and the two bookmakers hardly got out of jail to return to work before they were picked up again. Adam Kessel was very much disturbed. Fortunately, he had been tight fisted with his earnings, saving a fair-sized portion against the possibility of such a rainy day. Ad said good-by to Bauman and hung up his betting rolls.

A long rest gave Kessel the time he needed to view life in its proper perspective and also to collect many outstanding debts. In the course of his collection task, he fell heir to what might have been called an embryonic film exchange. One debt appeared to be

---

4 One of the classic examples was the Graphic Film Company. Capitalized on a shoestring to enter the rough-and-tumble world of movie-making, the shoestring broke within one month. It plunged into bankruptcy on a $74. note.

uncollectable in cash; the fellow was down on his luck. The only assets which he possessed were a few reels of film, and he talked Ad into accepting these to settle the account. Kessel knew nothing about motion pictures, but was impressed with their potential. Kessel provided the financial backing for the operation, and he and his debtor went into business. It soon became apparent to Adam Kessel that an entire new vista in life had opened its doors to him. Here was a way to make a good deal more money with fewer risks and no pesky police to take the fun out of life.

Looking up his former partner, Kessel found Charles Bauman still operating a prosperous tip service for bettors. But Bauman showed little interest in his friend's new endeavor. To assuage Charlie's doubts, Adam established a sub-exchange in Bauman's place of business and provided a man to service the accounts.[5] According to Kessel in an interview given many years later, prosperity beyond Bauman's wildest dreams followed. He cleared $210 at the end of the first week and changed his mind completely. Within a month his share had risen to $1,000 weekly, and Charles Bauman quickly became a full-fledged partner.

The very prosperity which befell their little operation nearly caused a downfall. The exchange business was a large one and was growing by leaps and bounds. Although many of the exchange operators had banded together to form the Film Service Association, a sort of professional society with a code of ethics, sharp operators were at work. Duping of films was a favorite trick, as were price-cutting, rebating, bicycling,[6] and other practices. Many exchange men resorted to such tactics in an effort to hinder their competition while fostering the growth of their own business. When Kessel and Bauman began to outstrip their friends and business associates in sales, a move was made to cut off their supply of licensed product. Nothing so angered friendly competitors as the growing prosperity of a rival.

[5] This brought Charles Kessel into the operation. Charles was to play a prominent role in his brother's future activities, but he always remained in the background, preferring to stay out of public view.

[6] The practice of renting one film and showing it in two theaters, transporting it by bicycle and avoiding the second rental fee.

The two former bookmakers did not react kindly to what they considered to be an underhanded trick and decided to retaliate by going into the production business. If they could not buy the product, Kessel and Bauman were determined to make it themselves. Hiring Fred Balshofer, who possessed a camera which the Edison people did not know existed, they shot a couple of short and simple films. Both were successful, and their favorable reception by exhibitors led to a meeting with Louis Burstein, an attorney.[7] During a hearty luncheon, they decided to incorporate, and thus the Bison Company came into being. Charles Inslee of Biograph was brought into the fold as a dramatic expert, and the Bison brand was off and running.

Not only were Kessel and Bauman out to fill their own exchange shelves with film; they offered their productions to others. Much to their surprise, the two found that an incredible demand existed. To the two gamblers, the ensuing profits were out of this world. According to Balshofer, a one-reel offering which cost $200 to produce brought in returns of $1,500 or even more in just a short time. No doubt about it, Kessel and Bauman had struck the mother lode. By 1910, they were deeply involved in the industry. The New York Motion Picture Company had been formed as a kind of holding company, Bison was big business, and Kessel and Bauman had a large interest in the formation of the original Reliance Company.[8]

To protect their varied interests from the Motion Picture Patents Company (the licensed film trust), Kessel and Bauman allied themselves with Carl Laemmle's Motion Picture Sales and Distributing Company at an early date. When this organization collapsed from internal stresses, they continued the alliance with Laemmle by joining his Universal Film Manufacturing Company

[7] Later known as Louis Burston, Burstein would soon form his own independent companies to produce. He is best remembered today for the King Bee Company which exploited Chaplin's keenest imitator, Billy West, and for Burston Productions, the serial unit which starred Francis Ford after World War I.

[8] The Bison Company was located in the West and produced frontier and Indian pictures. Reliance went into business in the East on October 22, 1910, to produce dramas. Stanner E. V. Taylor wrote the scripts, Eugene Sanger directed, and Max Schneider turned the camera. Marion Leonard, James Kirkwood, Arthur V. Johnson, and Henry B. Walthall were the first players.

when it began business on June 8, 1912.[9] As the driving force behind the new combine, Laemmle was elected president, but it was Charles Bauman who had actively lined up the needed support for him. However, Bauman and Kessel were suspicious of Laemmle, and on June 27, the New York Motion Picture Company withdrew from Universal.

This was made known officially when Kessel and Bauman notified two exchanges that Universal would no longer handle their films. Hereafter, the only place to obtain the New York Motion Picture Company's product would be from their four Empire exchanges. Now, everyone concerned realized the importance of this product to the Universal program and its success. The Bison pictures made in the West by Thomas Ince, along with the Eastern Reliance films, were a large factor in the growth of Laemmle's venture. Kessel and Bauman were proud of their films, and they, along with the creative talent which they had hired, put out the best possible product that a reasonable financial expenditure could make.

Laemmle was not to take this body blow to his authority without fighting back. Within hours after hearing the news, Universal asked for and received an injunction prohibiting the withdrawal. A warning went out to all exchanges that buying from the Empire exchanges would be in defiance of the court order. Universal sent a nicely phrased telegram to Fred Balshofer, relieving him immediately of all duties as Western general manager. It further ordered him to obey the wishes of one W. G. Gilmore of Nestor, who was on his way to assume control. As the New York office politely explained, it could not be certain where Balshofer stood in this dispute, thus the decision had been made in favor of a man whose loyalty was not open to question. Shortly after, Balshofer was contacted by David Horsley of Nestor's New York office. Horsley intended to come west to take charge, and was bringing William Swanson of the Rex brand with him.

[9] Universal was formed by combining Imp, Rex, Nestor, Powers, Champion, Republic, and the New York Motion Picture Company.

When Tom Ince heard the news, he immediately sided with Kessel and Bauman, and not only because they were paying his salary. Ince was highly disgusted with the manner in which Universal's home office had been treating some of his films. An autocrat on the lot, he was not accustomed to having his finished product re-edited, an offense of which the New York Universal people were all too often guilty.

Gilmore arrived in camp and as his first act, fired Fred Mace and a number of less important people. This infuriated Balshofer, who bodily threw the Nestor man off the Bison lot and rescinded all of his orders. Puzzled at the outset, Balshofer had quickly made a decision. He was not about to watch a carefully built organization destroyed by the whims of a clod who was interested only in the outcome of an executive power struggle. The situation became tense as the Nestor and Bison lots took on the appearance of armed camps, and each group threatened the other with the use of force.

Back in New York City, the Universal forces attempted to seize the property of the New York Motion Picture Company. Fortunately for Kessel and Bauman, a friendly stenographer phoned ahead, and they were prepared to resist Mark Dintenfass and his men. A small riot resulted but failed to achieve Dintenfass' ends. Pat Powers, unsatisfied with such a gross failure, organized a night raid which included gunplay. This was also unsuccessful. By June 29, cooler heads had prevailed, and the entire problem was dumped into the lap of the court, where legal confusion took over.

By October, the court had made its decision. Kessel and Bauman settled by giving up the Bison brand name, along with $17,000 in cash. In return, they were allowed to withdraw from the Universal combine. Both sides claimed victory, but from that date, the films which bore the Bison trade-mark failed to achieve the measure of distinction which the Ince pictures had possessed, and the Bison name did not fare well under Universal auspices.

Within a month after leaving Universal, Kessel and Bauman announced that they were to join the Mutual Film Corporation on July 29, 1912. Mutual had been formed by the group of dissidents who were once part of Laemmle's Sales Company and had caused its dissolution. Harry Aitken, John R. Freuler, Samuel S. Hutchison, and Charles J. Hite had decided to put Universal in its place. They first announced the formation of their new distribution unit and then went looking for money to finance the venture. It was found on Wall Street in the pockets of Crawford Livingston and Otto Kuhn.

When Kessel and Bauman aligned themselves with Mutual, they sold their four exchanges to the fledgling distribution firm and promised to deliver a minimum of six reels of completed film weekly. Aitken and Freuler, who owned the Majestic brand, purchased control of the Carlton Motion Picture Laboratories which produced the Reliance films for Kessel and Bauman. This left the former gamblers with their New York Motion Picture Company and quite a bit of cash and stock. Broncho, Kay Bee, and Domino brands became the trade-marks of their new product. Thus, the industrious pair had managed quite a coup. They had freed themselves from Carl Laemmle, raised cash by ridding themselves of the unwanted exchanges, and secured a new releasing arrangement which promised to be much more profitable. Mutual lacked but one thing for a fully diversified program; the time was ripe to form a new company and produce comedies.

Legend has it that Kessel and Bauman looked up Sennett to collect a gambling debt and were conned by the enterprising young man into establishing Keystone to collect their money. Nothing could be further from the truth, but this story has been long accepted. It is true that Sennett had a great liking for the ponies, but Kessel and Bauman had not retained their old line of work. Neither had taken a bet for four years. They were both clever operators, and as soon as the exchange business had proved itself to Bauman's satisfaction, Kessel had insisted that they break with the past completely. It seems merely to have been Sennett's good fortune to lunch at Luchow's restaurant on Fourteenth Street that particular day in August, 1912.

Sennett was now a director in his own right, heading a profitable unit at Biograph. From small roles and scenarios in 1909, he had

27

moved to leading parts in 1910 and direction in 1911. He stepped into the director's shoes with *Comrades,* a full-reel comedy of March 11, 1911, in which he shared the leading honors with Dell Henderson. When the front office saw this film, Sennett was finally given a comedy unit of his own. He was to function as director and actor at $50 weekly. The new director began to gather around him a crew which included Eddie Dillon, Vivian Prescott, Mabel Normand, Fred Mace, and Ford Sterling. His unit became a tightly knit organization in which everyone was free to contribute, and informal discussions were the order of the day.

In 1912, Sennett made *One-Round O'Brien,* a comedy about a punchy boxer. Dell Henderson had sold the story to Biograph on Sennett's recommendation and had received a $15 check for it. The plot revolved around a boxer who maneuvered his opponents against a canvas backdrop, behind which stood his accomplice who delivered the *coup de grâce* with a hammer. This was just the sort of roughhouse knockabout comedy which seemed to inspire Sennett, and he worked hard to make the production a success. Biograph raised his salary to $65 after seeing the returns brought in by this film. Fred Mace, the rotund comic who had played with Mack in *A Chinese Honeymoon* years before, had the lead and greatly enhanced his reputation with this single role.[10]

It was about this time that a streetcar conductor came into Sennett's life. When Henry Lehrman heard that Biograph paid $5 a day (and a Biograph working day could be only a few hours for an actor), he decided that movies were for him. Looking the situation over carefully, Henry came to the conclusion that experts were needed in the business. Where did experts who were well versed in the picture industry come from? France. No matter that Lehrman was a native of Vienna. With a newly acquired French accent, Henry applied for a job with Biograph. Introducing himself as M. Henri Lehrman, late of Paris and Pathé Frères, he sought to enlighten the American film industry on the

---

10 Mace worked with the Sennett unit at Biograph and then quit to join Imp. Thus, he was caught in the crossfire between Universal and the New York Motion Picture Company.

Ford Sterling in his famed Dutch makeup as the leader of *The Ragtime Band* (1913). Sterling's popularity in the early Keystones won him fame as one of the leading comics of his day.

Mabel Normand, the darling of the Keystone comedies, in a gag shot about 1914.

*Courtesy Academy of Motion Picture Arts and Sciences*

newest in methods and techniques, choosing Biograph as the first company to benefit from his "wide and varied" experience.

D. W. Griffith was not impressed by the phony French accent, but he did need help at that particular time and so Lehrman was placed on the payroll. In his very first role before the camera, Lehrman put everything he had into his work in the form of a bone-crushing fall. When informed that the camera had not caught the action, the zealous imposter hustled back into position, waited until the cameraman had framed the scene, and then repeated the fall. In this way he distinguished himself with a willingness to do anything for money, and Griffith nicknamed the fraudulent Frenchman "Pathé," a name that stayed with Lehrman for years. The new actor showed an affinity for comedy and soon became a part of the new Sennett unit.

Sennett's crew turned out a number of quick films using thin plots. Sennett conceived the idea of two daffy sleuths in *$500.00 Reward* (a release of August 21, 1911), and later comedies expanded the adventures of these popular characters. Sennett and Fred Mace played the leading roles as a pair of Sherlock Holmeses whose investigations led only to trouble. Although freewheeling and high spirited to a point, the Biograph comedies made by Sennett did not completely reflect his basic views on comedy. While his ideas were still in the formative stage, they were considered to be too radical by Biograph, and he was leashed as closely as possible to a standard formula. Sennett was bursting with ideas which brought nothing but frowns from the front office. Fortunately, the films he directed were welcomed by exhibitors, and Sennett kept a close eye on the accounting department. As soon as he felt it safe to do so, Mack asked for a raise and his salary went up to $75 weekly.

This was the state of his affairs when Kessel and Bauman met him that August day. It is not a matter of record as to who started the conversation, although Terry Ramsaye claimed that the two approached Sennett first.[11] Kessel and Bauman were not the small-

11 In his *A Million and One Nights* (Simon and Schuster, 1926).

time operators that Sennett intimated in his autobiography,[12] nor was Mack the insignificant director that Ramsaye made him out to be. Sennett had a growing reputation in the industry; Kessel and Bauman were wealthy executives heading a prominent film company, and it is likely that they had given some thought to his employment while narrowing the field of possible choices. They had been thinking for some time of expanding their operations into the field of comedy production, and once they joined Mutual, they found that a real need existed within the organization. Mutual contained no companies equipped to produce comedies, and such were necessary if the Mutual program was to take business away from Universal and General Film. With an excess of cash which was not earning its keep, Kessel and Bauman were searching for someone like Sennett. Since he was not a celebrity, he would not cost a fortune to acquire. On the other hand, his experience at Biograph was varied and successful enough to merit his consideration by the two former gamblers.

The Keystone Film Company was announced to the trade on August 12, 1912. It was established as a separate and distinct entity, having no official connection with any other motion-picture company, but owned by the New York Motion Picture Company. Kessel and Bauman put up the necessary money[13] and took the top offices of president and treasurer, respectively. Sennett contributed the talent and was given a one-third interest in the firm plus a salary of $100 weekly. It was also agreed that this would be adjusted as soon as Keystone had proven itself, for Tom Ince was receiving $300 at the time. Sennett also assumed the title of managing director, sometimes referred to as director-general. Over the years, film addicts and the general public alike have been under the mistaken impression that Mack Sennett owned the Keystone Film Company. While he guided the destiny of actual production, Kessel and Bauman held a rather close rein on the purse strings and decided how much Sennett could spend for various

---

[12] *King of Comedy* (Doubleday, 1954). This is interesting reading, but a disjointed and often unreliable source for serious study.
[13] Variously reported as being a sum between $2,500 and $3,000.

purposes.[14] They also took charge of the studio and its expansion program.

Legend has it that Sennett made pictures in New York City before going to California. This is an improbability, if not an impossibility, in view of the fact that only sixteen days elapsed between the decision to form the Keystone Film Company and the arrival of Sennett and Mabel Normand in Los Angeles on August 28.[15] All evidence indicates that the story of the New York production and Sennett's disasters with a Russian cameraman is nothing more than the product of some press agent's overactive imagination.

Once the agreement with Kessel and Bauman was made legal, Sennett had a great deal to do. Fred Mace was waiting on the Coast. Refusing a reinstatement by Imp, Mace was now on the payroll of the New York Motion Picture Company. Sennett's problems involved lining up a cast of comedians to work with him, setting up some form of workable organization, and gathering what equipment he needed to operate a production company.

Mack Sennett's fondest dreams had finally come true. At the age of thirty-four, he owned a partial interest in a motion-picture company, with total authority over scripts and the finished footage. He could experiment to his heart's desire with comic policemen and his other ideas about comedy. All that Kessel and Bauman asked of him was a steady flow of films that made money. He was to give them more than just that; Sennett was to give the two a product that would make fortunes for all involved, as well as a name that would forever be synonymous with silent-screen comedy. Unwittingly, he was to create a pandemonium on the silver screen that would one day draw raves from critics as a new art form—low

---

14 In all fairness to Kessel and Bauman, it should be pointed out that they rarely interfered with Sennett when it came to money matters. Sennett became accustomed to using them as his excuse in salary discussions with his players. Extravagant salary demands were kicked upstairs to Mutual, for the production contract with the distributor determined in effect the salaries paid. Kessel and Bauman could always say to Mutual, "If you wish to continue so and so's pictures, we must have more per foot."

15 Especially if Sennett himself is to be believed. In his autobiography he claimed that after the meeting with Kessel and Bauman, "We talked for days." Again, fiction seems to make a better story. Contemporaries who worked with him reject this story.

slapstick—whose form, content, and meaning would be discussed by the intellectuals for years to come. Mack Sennett was about to set the world of make-believe on its ear with something old, something new, something borrowed, and something outlandishly different—the Keystone comedy.

# 3. And a Legend Begins

Sᴇɴɴᴇᴛᴛ ᴀʀʀɪᴠᴇᴅ in Los Angeles on August 28.[1] With him was his star comedienne, Mabel Normand. Fred Mace was there to meet them, and Ford Sterling joined the three shortly. Sennett had a great deal of work to do. Kessel and Bauman had turned over the former Bison studio in Edendale for Keystone use. Deserted since the fracas over the withdrawal from Universal, the studio badly needed attention, which Sennett was unable to give it at the time. The equipment on hand was inventoried and a list of needs drawn up to be sent back to New York.

At this point, facts destroy forever one of the favorite legends concerning Sennett's arrival in Los Angeles. In his autobiography, Sennett even repeated a story which had been told many times over the years. According to this legend, a Shriners' Parade was the first sight to greet the new arrivals when they stepped from the train in Los Angeles. Sennett is said to have decided to take advantage of the parade setting, and dispatched Henry Lehrman to a near-by dime store to buy a baby doll. Ford Sterling supposedly put on a

[1] This was not his first trip to California, as other authors have suggested. Sennett was in Los Angeles as early as 1910 as a member of D. W. Griffith's winter company. During this stay, he became well acquainted with the city and the semirural area called Hollywood long before either came to be acknowledged as the motion-picture center of the world.

long overcoat when told to "make like an actor." Mabel grabbed the doll and ran up the street clutching the sleeves of various marchers in an effort to elicit an embarrassed response. She was followed by Ford in his overcoat, who engaged a Shriner in a loud argument. The police arrived and chased the comedians away; Sennett and his cameraman left in the other direction. As Mack told the story, they all went straight to Edendale, shot connecting scenes, and shipped the finished film off to New York City.

This is pure fancy, without any basis in fact. A search through the files of Los Angeles papers of this period fails to locate any mention of such a parade, which would certainly have been a newsworthy item. *Stolen Glory*, a Keystone released in October, 1912, included a G.A.R. parade, and the synopsis, as presented by Davide Turconi in his *Mack Sennett*, credits such a scene to the film. However, it was a staged affair, not the spontaneous event as related by Gene Fowler in his *Father Goose* and later repeated by Sennett. Through the years, film historians have harked back to the story of this supposed first Keystone comedy. They also often name *At Coney Island* as the initial offering of the new company, overlooking the fact that such a plot would hardly fall within a film bearing that title. Sennett mentioned Henry Lehrman as having taken part in the incident, but Lehrman did not arrive with the first contingent of Keystoners. It was the end of September before he arrived in California to join the company.

To set the record straight, it should be noted that a Biograph release of July, 1912, *The Would-Be Shriner*, did make use of a Shriners' Parade in Los Angeles. The most logical explanation is that someone twisted the facts relating to the two films over the years, added a large dash of fiction, and passed it out to an unsuspecting and gullible public. Human-interest items are always welcome, and this story fell into that category. *The Would-Be Shriner* was one of the final films which Sennett made for Biograph, and was undoubtedly made during the winter of 1911–12, when Sennett was in Los Angeles with a Biograph crew. He played a prominent role in the film, and its story line in the *New York Dramatic Mirror* credits him as portraying "Hank," a character

Alice Davenport hands Mabel Normand her walking papers as Chester Conklin (*left*) and Charlie Chase (*center*) look on, in this scene from *Mabel's New Job* (1914).

Ford Sterling is caught in the act in
*His Father's Footsteps* (1915).

*Courtesy Academy of Motion Picture Arts and Sciences*

name assigned to him by Biograph, who did not publicize its actors' names at the time.

Many other stories about Sennett and Keystone have been distorted over the years. It is logical to assume that they were repeated so often that Sennett himself came to believe them. This situation often arises when interviewing motion-picture actors who were popular in the silent period. Many of the stories that they tell read straight from the fan magazines. Even when presented with solid facts which chronologically destroy the basis for their story, they tend to cling to it tenaciously. These actors attempt to discredit the facts, to the extent of denying that a certain company was in existence at the time of their story.

Soon after arriving in Los Angeles, Sennett contacted the scenario editor of Kay Bee. Richard V. Spencer handled the scripts and had just been promoted to general script supervisor for the New York Motion Picture Company, responsible for all stories. Spencer hired Jessie Booth to work under him as story editor for the Broncho brand. Karl Coolidge was hired from the Ammex Company to move over to Edendale and assume the position of Keystone story editor.[2] Coolidge had been very successful in writing and selling scripts on a free-lance basis before joining Ammex. A man with a highly developed sense of humor, he appeared to be just the person to take over the story responsibilities at Keystone. When Spencer received word from New York that he had been promoted and could hire two more people, he went immediately to Coolidge and offered him the job. Ammex was not in very sound condition and Coolidge was restless. The offer appealed to the frustrated writer, and he accepted without hesitation. This left Spencer as editor of Kay Bee with supervision responsibilities for the other two brands.

Spencer introduced Sennett to Coolidge, and the three men held an impromptu conference. Sennett made it clear that he expected to exercise final judgment over scripts, even though he felt scripts to be unnecessary. During his last two years at Biograph, many

2 Coolidge was to become a well-known script writer in the twenties and is still remembered by many fans for his fascinating script of the first Art Acord serial, *The Moon Riders*.

of his best comedies had been shot off the cuff, improvising as he went along.

Now we must backtrack just a bit to look at the first roster of Keystone players. D. W. Griffith had taken a company of Biograph players west for the 1911–12 winter season. When Griffith was ready to return to the East, the popular Fred Mace decided to stay in California and left Biograph for work at Imp. This lasted only a short time before the problems between Universal and Kessel and Bauman erupted into threatened violence, and Mace, caught in the middle, was left without a job. As soon as Sennett confirmed the founding of Keystone, Mace was notified and happily agreed to rejoin his old friend and comrade in the new venture. He proved to be most valuable to the firm.

As a boy, Ford Sterling had joined John Robinson's circus in his home town of La Crosse, Wisconsin. When the circus left La Crosse, Ford went with it as an extra clown. He worked up to feature billing as "Keno, the Boy Clown" before leaving the circus world for a stock and repertoire company. Sterling played roles in every type of show from *Uncle Tom's Cabin* to *Julius Caesar.* The experience which he gained eventually helped Ford to break into musical comedy in the Broadway play *Side Walk Chatter.*

In late 1911, Sterling joined the Biograph Company, where he met and became friendly with Mack Sennett. Sennett used him in several comedies, and Sterling was ready for the big move to Keystone in 1912. A tall and athletic fellow, Sterling's screen comedy was of a broad and expressive nature and made generous use of acrobatics. Contrary to the popular belief, Ford did not acquire the so-called "Dutch" make-up (consisting of tuft beard and moustache) at the outset. He appeared in many early Keystones with just the pencil moustache which he sometimes wore in real life. His make-up in these films consisted mainly of an exaggerated eye shading.

The third and most important of the group was Mabel Normand. Her birthplace has been given as Boston, Providence, or Atlanta, depending upon the writer. Mack Sennett had no success in 1951 when he attempted to locate baptismal records which would clear up the doubts. According to Sennett, she was of French extraction; the family name was really Normand. Since she was a sincere Catholic, born of a practicing Catholic family in 1894, it is difficult to believe that no records at all exist. Somewhere, in some dusty church archive, there must be a slip of paper which would clear up the mystery, but it has never been located.

Her formal education was not extensive, for the family never prospered. The father, a would-be piano player, had traveled up and down the East Coast playing in vaudeville houses and wherever else a piano player could make a dime. This type of life continued until he finally settled in Staten Island and gave up the piano. Mabel went to work at an early age to supplement the family income. Her first job was in the pattern department of a magazine that catered to women. At age thirteen, her physical development was that of a mature woman, and the head of the pattern department realized that she was pretty enough to pose for artists. He introduced her to Carl Kleinschmidt, a noted illustrator, and Mabel began posing for fifty cents an hour.

Kleinschmidt was so pleased with the natural ability and grace of his new model that he introduced her to many other artists. Before long, Mabel was posing for Charles Dana Gibson and James Montgomery Flagg, two of the generation's most famous portrayers of feminine pulchritude. In the next three years, she became well established in the modeling profession and at the suggestion of a friend, she decided to try pictures in 1911.

After a few roles in Vitagraph films, Mabel applied for work at Biograph. Fortunately for her future, Wilfred Lucas needed a girl with nice-looking legs. The job was hers and so was the $10 she earned for a day-and-night shooting session. Lucas was behind schedule on the film and paid the cast overtime to finish it. It was here that she met Mack Sennett, who was still only an actor with high hopes. The two became friends, and soon Sennett began to confide many things to the diminutive beauty. By 1911, Sennett had acquired enough nerve to buy Mabel an inexpensive ring, and she became his girl. It was one of his everlasting regrets that he never married Mabel Normand.[3]

What is important here is that when Sennett was given the Keystone Film Company, it was not a difficult task to talk Mabel into joining his little group of players. For Sennett, it was another stroke of good fortune. Mabel Normand went on to acquire a reputation as the one female comic genius of the silent films, a feminine counterpart of Charles Chaplin. No one who knew her seemed able to explain her genius, but all agreed that it was there. A born mimic with a broad sense of humor, her popularity with both friends and fans was boundless. Perhaps a great deal of this success was in the fact that unlike other comediennes of the time, she did not strain for effects. They came naturally by an infinite number of tiny and shifting facial expressions that more than adequately conveyed what she was trying to tell her audiences. In this respect, her bubbling personality dominated her on-screen performance.

Although not beautiful by modern standards, Mabel Normand was able to project a fresh, clean, and innocent appearance through the tattered clothes she wore in many Keystones. She was also able to impersonate a rough and tough hussy. Herein was her chief value to the early Keystones—she could portray any role with a grace and ease that made the audiences believe in her.

This was the original Keystone troupe. Sennett functioned as director and put in numerous appearances before the camera during the first year. A supporting cast of players, including Dot Farley, Victoria Forde, Alice Davenport, and Evelyn Quick, was

3 Mabel Normand was involved in the scandal concerning the unsolved murder of director William Desmond Taylor. Two years later, she was keeping company with millionaire Cortland S. Dines when her chauffeur, Joe Kelly, was found standing by the body of Dines with a pistol in his hand. The pistol was the property of Mabel, and Joe Kelly turned out to be an escaped convict named Horace Greer. Mabel's innocence was never questioned, but the headlines made it clear that her career was finished. She tried a comeback in the latter twenties in Hal Roach's "All-Star Series," but it failed to put her back on top. Married to Lew Cody, she entered the hospital in 1927 with double pneumonia. It was here that tuberculosis was discovered. By September, 1929, she was in Dr. Francis Pottenger's sanitarium in Monrovia. Desperately ill for six months, she died on February 23, 1930. She never knew that her husband suffered from heart disease; he passed away shortly after her. Some historians have suggested that she was a victim of narcotics addiction, which was a complicating factor in her last few years of life. They subscribe to the theory that Taylor was murdered when he tried to help her break the habit.

quickly brought together. The company went into production shortly after arriving in Los Angeles, and the Keystone program opened officially on September 23 with two split-reel comedies, *Cohen Collects a Debt* and *The Water Nymph*. A new reel containing two comedies appeared once a week through January, 1913.

The Keystone comedies were an immediate hit with exhibitors and fans alike. Everyone raved about them, and they quickly became the industry standard by which all other comedies were to be judged. Of course, the state of comedy films in the autumn of 1912 was indeed sad. Biograph was now out of the running; Selig and Lubin had never really been contenders. Only Vitagraph and Essanay were making comedies of value. Vitagraph's place in comedy history was assured by the films of a portly comedian, John Bunny. He was truly the first screen comic and so popular with audiences that he was mobbed several times by adoring fans on personal-appearance tours.

Most of the Essanays were turned out under the guiding hand of one E. Mason Hopper, nicknamed "Lightning" Hopper by his friends in recognition of his speed and skill at cartooning.[4] The Essanay comedies were mainly of the rural slapstick and situation variety. The "Snakeville" comedies were popular examples of homespun humor that made Margaret Joslin, Victor Potel, and Augustus Carney valued properties. Carney had his own characterization, "Alkali Ike," which was also founded on rural humor. Wallace Beery, the star of the "Sweedie" comedies, did an acceptable female impersonation in his series dealing with the misadventures of a Swedish maid.

The Keystone comedies had a style and character all their own. They moved with the rapidity of greased lightning, and the ridiculous characters that streaked across the screen immediately won the hearts of movie fans across the nation. For the most part, those

---

4 Hopper, a native of Enosburg, Vermont, came to the movies in 1911 from the stage. His specialty was a charcoal-sketching act, but he soon proved to be adept at writing and directing motion pictures. Today he is best remembered for his "Edgar" series which he directed for Goldwyn and for his work as director of the Hearst spectacle, *Janice Meredith*.

comedies produced by other firms were little more than aimless slapstick which brought laughs by means of their crude and often questionable taste, not by their inherent humor. A number of lesser producers merely set up their cameras on street corners and captured the unrehearsed antics of their comics, who were usually dressed as hobos or tramps.

But the Keystones were different, and surprisingly enough, when one examines the content of the early Keystones, some interesting patterns emerge. As the other face of tragedy, true comedy is separated from its brother by but a thin line. Visual humor made use of essentially tragic situations but stopped short of reaching the logical conclusion. In real life, a marital mix-up can only cause pain and dismay to those involved, but in the world of Keystone, nothing really tragic ever took place. The fantasy of such situations was a forerunner of the animated cartoons of the sound era. Bombs, bullets, and bludgeons were frequent props, yet no one was seriously injured and it was just good clean fun for the audiences.

Many early Keystones dealt with the pretensions of a society that was bent on elevating itself, but an equal number of the films' subjects would be heartily condemned today. The Jewish people were a regular target as in the "Cohen" series which Mace and Sterling made. There appeared quite a number of "colored folk" comedies, in which the Negro was made to appear as the butt of numerous jokes. *The Darktown Belle, Rastus and the Game Cock,* and *Father's Choice* all found the Keystone players in blackface and poking fun at the Negro stereotype of the day.

In the latter comedy, Mabel's father wanted her to marry a man whom he had chosen. She rebelled and ran away with her lover. Both were disguised as Negroes. Persuaded to attend the wedding, the father unsuspectingly acted as the best man, and the subtitles labeled the couple, "only a pair of coons."[5]

*A Double Wedding* was another example of the Keystone topic which would be taboo today, but which found great favor with

[5] Such crude taste was not unusual. In late 1914, Keystone produced *A Nigger Dice Game.* The title was fortunately changed just before release to *A Dark Lover's Play.*

audiences at the time. It concerned two weddings—one of a white couple and the other of two Negroes. The latter couple were mistaken by the "society swells" as their friends, for the colored couple got into the wrong car. The comedy centered upon the reactions of the actors in black face to the attentions lavished on them by the whites. Of course, the whole thing ended in a mad chase once the deception was discovered.

Other favorite Keystone themes included marital mix-ups where one couple flirted with another, unbeknown to their respective spouses. Police, parsons, and landlords came in for their share of Keystone comment. Widows and fathers also received the treatment, as did orchestras and salesmen. In short, the entire range of human affairs and its participants were grist for the Keystone mill.

An exceedingly popular theme was brought back to life with the reintroduction of the pair of dopey detectives. As we have seen, Sennett had used this characterization in a few Biograph films which met with much financial success, and less than six weeks after starting Keystone production, he and Fred Mace restored the detectives to the screen in *At It Again*.

Sterling handled the Jewish roles with ease, and Fred Mace filled the perfect stereotype of a fat Spaniard. The Spaniards and Italians received almost as much kidding as did the Jews and Negroes. Mabel naturally played in all the films, regardless of theme, and soon became known as "Keystone Mabel." Sennett directed the majority and acted in many. Whenever the story called for a country rube or a bumbling boob, Mack threw down his megaphone and walked in front of the camera. He filled either role with a fine degree of natural perfection, but in other parts, he was less successful. His pantomime was heavy and his histrionic range was questionable. Sennett often served to distract rather than add to a production, but he was the boss and if he wished to act, who was going to tell him otherwise?

Production at Keystone was hot and heavy. Sennett often boasted of turning out a completed half-reel comedy in one short day. Within a month after he began filming, Pathé Lehrman walked in looking for work and Sennett put him on the payroll.

Lehrman was acting and criticizing Sennett's direction the very same day. The two men were old friends, but Lehrman's personality was not calculated to let friendship interfere with his conception of how a picture should be made. It is therefore not surprising that when Keystone expanded to include a second unit, Lehrman was made its director.

Adam Kessel was pleased with the sales potential of the footage coming out of the Edendale studio and went west in November, 1912, to look over the possibilities of expanding the facilities. With him went "Doc" Willat, a laboratory expert and the technical chief of Kessel's growing empire. The two men conferred with Sennett and decided to expand the release schedule to two reels (or four comedies) per week beginning on February 6, 1913. Charles Avery and Betty Shade were hired for the second unit, which was to function under Lehrman.

# 4. Comedy, Keystone Style

THE KEYSTONE KOPS were Sennett's major contribution to Americana and to the American language. The Kops have come to symbolize an era in screen comedy, as well as any nonsensical action which takes place today. Practically every actor whose movie career began in the dawn of screen history has claimed to be one of the original Keystone Kops. So many have in fact claimed this distinction that in order to accommodate every claim, Sennett would have had to have hired a police force large enough for a city. As Mack recalled it in his autobiography, there were only seven—George Jesky, Bobby Dunn, Mack Riley, Charles Avery, Slim Summerville, Edgar Kennedy, and Hank Mann.

The truth of this will probably never be proven, for the Keystone Kops did not appear full blown on the screen. Rather, they emerged after a gradual evolution of the idea that Sennett had nurtured for years. The first recorded existence of a Kop picture from Keystone was the release of December 23, 1912, *Hoffmeyer's Legacy*. From this point on, one or more policemen were in nearly every comedy until April 24, 1913, when *The Bangville Police* appeared.

This hilarious single reel concerned the bucolic heroine who desired a calf for a playmate. (How simple life once was!) Deciding to surprise his daughter, father bought the animal in town and made arrangements to have it delivered without his daughter's knowledge. But as the deliverymen entered the barn, they were seen by the girl. She jumped to the conclusion that they were robbers and placed a frantic call to the local police. This set the stage for action on the part of the rural Kops and, piling into their dilapidated vehicle, the officers set off for the scene of the crime.

After numerous hilarious adventures en route, the automobile blew up and they finished the trip on foot. Arriving at the farmhouse, the police found the house doors bolted and practically ruined the entire property before clearing up the mistaken identity of the "burglars." The cause of law and order took a sound beating in this picture. The success of *The Bangville Police* tempted Mack to experiment further with the Kops in featured roles, culminating with the classic *In the Clutches of a Gang*, a full two-reel offering of January 27, 1914.

This thoroughly enjoyable film burlesqued the Kops on a kidnapping case. As Chief Teheezel, Ford Sterling led forth his hardy band to solve the crime. As might be suspected, they encountered every difficulty ever associated with Keystone. Deciding that the mayor was the culprit, the bungling Kops arrested him, but fortune smiled on them and the case solved itself without their stalwart assistance. It was one of the finest of the Keystone comedies.

By this time, the uniform had become standardized and Ford Sterling (now in Dutch make-up) was the nominal leader of the force—"nominal" because, as a group, the Kops paid very little attention to the commands given by their chief. Their on-screen antics were more or less a case of every man for himself. Otherwise sedate members of the audiences roared with laughter when these caricatures of suburban peace officers piled up in the waters of Eastlake Park or were flung in all directions across the Hollywood landscape in a valiant effort to remain with their speeding flivver.

Each new comic signed for the Keystones in 1913 was given a trial period in a Kop uniform. In this position, it was quite easy for Sennett to determine whether the man actually had what it took

The original Keystone Kops find themselves in a predicament which helped to create the classic Keystone legend.

*Courtesy Larry Edwards Bookshop*

Marital mix-ups were a favorite Keystone theme, and the tale of *Mabel, Fatty and the Law* (1915) was no exception.

to be a true Keystone comedian. If he had the stamina to stand up under the sometimes brutal punishment and still come across as being funny in Sennett's opinion, the man was retained. If not, the poor fellow had learned his lesson the hard way.

It is true that many of the Kop escapades were camera tricks, such as the classic patrol wagon that unloaded a preposterous number of bodies from a seemingly never-ending supply. Actually, as each man got out he disappeared down the road out of camera range and returned to the wagon while the camera was not running. Once again the film began to roll, and once more the bodies fell, stumbled, and plunged out into the street, giving the ridiculous illusion of one hundred Kops in a wagon designed for not more than ten. As the last man got out, the vehicle quite often collapsed on the spot.

It is equally true that there was a good deal of danger connected with the antics of the Keystone Kops. Insurance companies were hesitant to cover these actors, for the possibility of injury remained high. Of course, the Kops were the lowest on the scale of Keystone comedians and no doubles substituted for them. If these men couldn't do it, it couldn't be done. Running over rooftops, across the edge of buildings, falling up and down stairs—all were part of the stock-in-trade of a Kop.

A favorite stunt, and one which always drew a hearty laugh from the audience, was the Kop who was dragged down the street behind an apparently fast-moving automobile. Photographed with a camera operating at eight to twelve frames per second rather than the usual sixteen to twenty-four frames per second, the footage appeared to move very rapidly on screen. This gave the impression that the poor Kop was really taking a beating. Fans roared at the sight of such an indignity. Fortunately for the poor comic, there was a trick to it. Underneath the Kop was a pair of small roller-bearing wheels mounted on a small platform. This apparatus served to make the trip down the street less bruising. What was really difficult for the comic was the task of making it appear realistic by arm and leg movements as he progressed behind the slow-moving automobile. The additional speed provided by Keystone editing[1] made the sequence appear brutal and bone crushing. It was customary to remove every third or fourth frame during the preliminary cutting of certain sequences. This added to the speed on screen and also contributed to the jerky movement which we now think of as characteristic of a Keystone comedy.

Such escapades could give even the best comic a fair number of scrapes and bruises, but it must be remembered that these were knockabout comedians—men who were accustomed to taking such punishment. For the average citizen, such treatment would be disastrous, but the men who composed the Keystone police force were trained acrobats and tumblers. These men knew how to take falls in stride. The majority of them had taken severe bumps and bruises for years as a routine part of their everyday life. The life of a Keystone Kop was a step up the ladder for most of them. With any luck, their career could easily catch fire, moving them into the ranks of featured or starring comedians. It happened to a few.

Another of Sennett's contributions to the world of screen comedy was the chase. Every comedy—or so it seemed—had to end with a chase. If the director could think of no other way of winding up his reel, there was always the chase. This technique was borrowed from the French, but few Méliès or Pathé comedies ever had such organized and mannerly chases as Sennett staged. There were infinite varieties to choose from: the single chase involving two or more people or the "en masse" chase with two or more groups taking part. There was the man-animal chase, the animal-man chase, the man-vehicle chase, the vehicle-man chase. Also staged were animal-animal chases and vehicle-vehicle chases. A little imagination and the list would cover another entire page.

Regardless of type, the beauty about a Keystone chase was its style and precision.[2] All began in a somewhat orderly progression,

---

1 The method of interconnecting events with short scenes for the purpose of building suspense was known in the trade as "Biograph editing," and is attributed to D. W. Griffith. When applied in conjunction with the frame removal to comedy subjects after 1912, it was called "Keystone editing."

2 Although used several years before Keystone began, the chase had been overworked by American producers until it fell out of favor. In 1910, Dandy Films adver-

and the tempo increased as the length of the chase extended. Up hill, down hill, in and out of buildings (even through them), down city streets and country lanes, the Keystone comics chased each other. The real fun inherent in such a sequence came from the various indignities suffered by the pursuers and the pursued. Flowerpots, barrels, chicken coops, mud holes, flying bricks— anything at hand had its day.

The wild use of automobiles involved several elements. Chases were not shot off the cuff, as was the case with much comic byplay. They had to be carefully outlined and planned. Camera speed, editing, and trick photography all played a large role, but so did such ingenious things as a barrel of liquid soap and skilled racing drivers. Permission would be granted by the authorities to use a certain intersection for filming. There were even times when no one bothered to get permission. Liquid soap was then spread over the road, and the drivers took over at speeds of fifty miles an hour before applying their brakes. Planned havoc resulted and was captured on film.

The railroad crossing was another favorite playground of the Keystone chase. Death-defying danger always added an interesting element to the comic routine (especially if the comedians hammed it up at the same time), and audiences appreciated nothing better than a good rousing head-on crash. The services of a locomotive and its crew were rented for a day, and Keystone comics cavorted for the camera. One scene which always thrilled the fans was the stalled car with a train approaching rapidly from the distance beyond. Depending upon the requirement of the scene, the locomotive might plow through the car at high speed or it might come to a sudden stop before any harm could be done, frightening the audience but holding down the budget. In this case, it was a camera trick. The locomotive backed up from the car as fast as it could while the camera turned in reverse. When projected, the scene appeared to be just the opposite: a steaming bundle of iron high-

tised their ware as containing "no long drawn, agonizing chases over hill and dale." Keystone restored the technique to favor with its carefully planned and executed chases.

balling down the rail to a panic stop. This very effective technique was also used with automobiles and trolley cars. Copied by other producers, it met with great success down through the years.

Sennett always maintained that no director could be expected to join the company and stage a genuine Keystone chase immediately. All directors had to be a part of the operation before they could really experience the correct feeling. Viewing the imitations that other firms made gives one the impression that Sennett was correct in his theory. No matter how hard they tried, others were unable to duplicate the Keystone touch with any consistent degree of success. Sennett always preferred to promote directors from the ranks, if possible. This reasoning explained his early attitude toward new comics, who began with supporting roles until they proved themselves.

Keystone's last and perhaps best-remembered contribution to silent-screen comedy was the pie. Sennett told the story himself many times (and other writers have accepted it as the gospel) that Mable Normand threw the first pie into Ben Turpin's face as a casual stroke of genius. The other circumstances surrounding this discovery might well have been true, but Ben Turpin most certainly was not the recipient of the pastry. Turpin did not join Keystone until 1917, when his contract with Vogue had expired.

It is possible that a pie was thrown in an earlier comedy, but the first Keystone pie on record sailed into Roscoe Arbuckle's face in *A Noise From the Deep*, a release of July 17, 1913. Mabel Normand *was* the culprit who delivered the *coup de grâce*. Sennett knew a good thing when he saw it. A pie in the face, provided the recipient does not anticipate it, has no equal in slapstick comedy. It can reduce dignity to nothing in seconds.[3]

Del Lord became the most experienced pie-thrower on the lot. He often likened it to an art, requiring a sense of balance and form. The pie was not really thrown or heaved, although it appeared that way on screen. Actually, it was pushed forward into the air with a smooth follow-through. Lord maintained that six to eight

---

[3] It can also make a man rich. Witness "Soupy" Sales, the slapstick television comic. "Soupy" estimates that he has been hit with over 18,000 pies in his career; today he is a wealthy man.

feet was the maximum distance for a successful flight, although Chester Conklin still points to Roscoe Arbuckle, who could do it with either hand at ten feet.

Pies for throwing were not edible. Some were filled with paste, others with blackberries covered with whipped cream. The filling had to have a rather thick consistency in order to hold together during flight. Although they were used at first, ordinary custard pies did not have the necessary body nor did they photograph well. Any pie that sailed into camera range and did a figure eight before splashing into the unwary victim's face had to be a special one.[4]

The Keystone films gave a new meaning and dimension to the term "slapstick comedy." For many years, Sennett was considered to be the originator of such, but for once he refused to take the credit. His brand of humor derived directly from the French films of Méliès and Pathé, whose imaginative product in the period before 1912 made use of many of the elements soon to become a Keystone trade-mark. Slapstick comedy was an acknowledged French creation; Keystone's contribution was to add an American touch (taken from burlesque) and a form of refinement by combining ludicrous characters, costumes, and situations, making full use of camera and editing tricks and taking advantage of fake properties such as breakaway vases, bottles, removable room partitions, and the like.

Critics have remained in awe over the years at the supposed art to be found in the Keystone comedies. There was no preconceived art to a Keystone for its motivation was money, pure and simple. Sennett turned out comedies on an assembly line to make people willingly part with their money for the privilege of laughter. There was no thought at the time of Keystone comedy deriving from classic ballet, or any of the other nonsense handed out to the public by latter-day "authorities." But it is also true that there was a certain amount of pacing within each film which can be interpreted as an art form. This was a prerequisite of comedy—screen, stage, or otherwise.

Any comic worth his stuff knew that tempo was important.

---

4 This was done by an expert fly-caster atop a stepladder and out of camera range.

One of Roscoe Arbuckle's favorite descriptions of screen comedy was, "The gag must follow the plant as closely as possible." The plant was the cause; the gag was the effect. What Arbuckle meant was simply that very little time should be wasted after the cause had been revealed. When the audiences were shown one of the Keystone comics fooling around with a gas tank and a lighted match, they knew at once what was about to take place. Arbuckle's formula called for the explosion to happen within seconds. If too long a delay existed between cause and effect, the audience had too much time to anticipate, and when it finally occurred, the gag's impact was diminished.

Gags had to be properly spaced in order to give the audience a chance to laugh, recover, and laugh again. Too lengthy a delay between gags meant silence in the theater, and silence was fatal to a comic's career. If the delay was too short, the audience would miss gag number two while still laughing at gag number one. No comic used his best material first—this would have been occupational suicide. Instead, the gags had to progress in intensity, building the audience up as the film unreeled. The sharp editing which Sennett learned under Griffith was a means of helping to pace a film properly.

The early Keystones should properly be considered as farces, not comedies. Farce only becomes comedy when some degree of characterization dominates the plot. Few of the Keystones possessed much in the way of characterization during 1912–14. For the most part, the films were shot informally, and such impromptu filming does not lend itself easily to development of characterization. Sennett believed in making use of any available opportunities. One day in January, 1913, he learned that Tom Ince was doing a Civil War picture with many extras and lots of gunpowder. Ford Sterling and a crew were sent over to Ince's location, and *The Battle of Who Run* resulted. Taking advantage of Ince's elaborate staging in this manner allowed Keystone to advertise the full-reel comedy as an extravaganza in terms of cost, extras, and production values. Actually, its cost did not exceed the average Keystone.

Comedy replaced farce in only a half-dozen films during 1913.

March saw the release of the first of many famed Keystones, *At Twelve O'Clock*. This was the beginning of the Keystone comic melodrama, a burlesque on the heavy drama of the stage and of rival film producers. Mabel Normand played the heroine who refused to marry the Italian villain, Fred Mace. The first half of this single reel was carefully devoted to building characterization, and then everything broke loose.

The rejected lover bound lovely Mabel tightly in front of an old grandfather's clock which had been timed to fire a bullet at the stroke of twelve. This was to teach Mabel the price of rejection. The remainder of the film was devoted to Sennett's efforts to save her with a magnet tied to a pole. Thrust in an open window, it moved the hands back just in the nick of time. Not hearing the shot, Mace re-entered the room to discover that the clock was slow. Setting the hands ahead, he left again to await the sound that would signal success. This scene was repeated with several variations until help finally arrived to capture Mace and free Mabel. The remarkable acceptance of this film brought forth several others in the same vein.

*Mabel's Awful Mistake* was a classic burlesque (for its day) of the heavy melodramas of the time. It was the story of the rascally bigamist who proposed marriage to the trusting and innocent country girl. Sweet Mabel accepted the offer, but when she learned the truth and started to return home, she wound up tied to a planing table in the sawmill. Only the arrival of her rube lover (Sennett) saved the day and Mabel.

*Barney Oldfield's Race for a Life* involved more dramatic action. Oldfield was the noted speed demon of 1912, and he agreed to ham it up for the Keystone cameras. The plot had Mabel refuse Ford Sterling, only to end up tied to the railroad track as Ford stole a locomotive to do her in. Sennett, again playing her country lover, and Oldfield staged a race with the train which included wild driving, bullets, and bombs. Naturally, the heroes beat the train and foiled Sterling's plot, but only after a great deal of suspense had been interwoven with the humor.

In the same manner, Sennett parodied Griffith's *The Miser's*

*Heart* with *A Life in the Balance*. Each of these films was well received by audiences who knew at once that Keystone was kidding the daylights out of their favorite form of screen entertainment. There seemed to be a moral to these early Keystone comedies that reached the audiences without too much thinking on their part. The heroine was sweet, young, and innocent. The more education and manners a man possessed, the more likely he was to be a black-hearted villain. The hero was usually slow witted and somewhat ignorant, a laughable character.

Audience laughter at the Keystones of 1912–13 came not so much from the story as from the action involved. The simple stories were nothing more than a frame on which to hang gag after gag. Whereas the great successes of Keaton, Lloyd, and Chaplin were to come from films with reasonably sound stories as backdrops, the early Keystones had no time nor any need for such. As a matter of fact, few 1913 comedies were afforded the luxury of a strong and lineal story line. In this particular respect, Keystone was little different from its competition.

The difference came in the action. *Cohen Saves the Flag* had the following story outline: Cohen and Goldberg were rivals for the hand of Mabel. They both entered military service—Cohen as a private and Goldberg as an officer. Since Mabel had appeared to favor Cohen, Goldberg decided to get rid of him forever. To this end, he assigned Cohen to a suicide mission. The hero's true colors appeared when he decided to desert rather than to get himself killed. In the wild melee that followed, he wandered into the battle zone and inadvertently saved the flag. Acclaimed a hero by the soldiers in the field, he was captured by Goldberg, who had followed him to make certain that he was killed. The deceitful friend took Cohen back to the rear and was about to execute him when the field soldiers arrived, singing praises for Cohen's heroism.

The laughter was sprinkled throughout, but its heaviest concentration came in the scenes where Cohen and Goldberg tried to outwit each other, and in the flight of the cowardly Cohen as he blundered into battle rather than away from it. Heavy pantomime predominated throughout. The finale, which included tearful

A portion of the Keystone Studio in Edendale, California, in 1912. Note the translucent roof and sides which diffused the direct sunlight for outdoor filming. On cloudy days, the roof section rolled back and the sides were raised for additional illumination.

*Courtesy Academy of Motion Picture Arts and Sciences*

Charlie Chaplin finds he can afford to treat Charlie Murray to a drink in *Mabel's Married Life* (1914), but will he?

scenes of both Mabel and Cohen begging Goldberg not to carry out the execution, was the topper and brought gales of chuckles as Cohen's supposed bravery was revealed to his unbelieving ears. The mood changed abruptly from sadness to joyful spite as the tables were turned on the scheming Goldberg. This formula had been repeated many times by the Keystones with successful results, but change was in the air as 1913 gave way to 1914. The public pulse was in the process of quickening, and among comedy producers, Sennett's finger was most firmly attached to that pulse.

Sennett had a most favorable sense of humor. More than anything else, this represented the key to Keystone's early success. With his previous training in and around burlesque, Sennett knew what was funny to the man on the street. He could tell by viewing the rushes whether or not the day's footage would meet with audience approval. While he was still active in all phases of production during 1913, Sennett was able to keep a tight rein on the output. Footage that did not make him laugh was discarded or shot over to include the suggested variations. Footage that did make him happy was carefully timed for tempo, and if suggestions were in order, they were carried out.

His ideas of comedy, though still developing, had several interesting aspects. First of all, he believed that movies must *move*, a throwback to his days with Griffith. He firmly believed in the "hub theory," as he termed it. A central idea constituted the hub, and natural developments arising from the idea formed the spokes. As he often said in interviews, "Give us an idea; we'll add the action."

Sennett was perhaps the first comedy producer to grasp the idea that if one of a kind is funny, two can be funnier. If one Kop could be a scream, twelve Kops could be a riot. In putting his ideas into practice, Sennett relied on the time-tested truisms of burlesque— perilous situations, coincidence, disguise, contrast, sentiment, etc. The incongruous played a large role in the Keystone ability to provoke laughter. Audiences roared with tears in their eyes at the sight of a lovely young girl doting on a ludicrous old man, who quite often was fat, bald, and ugly. It is interesting to note that nearly every leading lady in the Keystones was attractive; few of the men filled the bill as handsome lovers.

Although the finished product did not prove it in every instance, Sennett stood firm in his belief that it was not possible to be comical unless one was also logical. The logic that flowed through some Keystones was often of a perverted nature, and examination of many others defies an attempt to find the logic. However, one of the cardinal tenets of Keystone production crews was: Be logical.

It is likely that a formal education would have spoiled his precious gift, for Sennett seems to have been genuinely representative of the audiences that viewed his films. The reviewers and critics of the day reported his pictures to be vulgar, but still the demand for Keystones rose. A touch of vulgarity which offended sensitive and educated people was exactly what appealed to the average moviegoer of 1913. The earthy sense of humor prevalent in the burlesque and vaudeville houses touched each fan's existence, and he recognized it for what it was—life. Although often crude and vulgar in itself, life was seldom as fantastic as Keystone made it appear to be, but in exaggeration there is humor.

# 5. The First Year

IN 1913, there were more than 20,000 theaters in the United States. Each and every night, 96,000,000 feet of film ran through the projectors across the nation. Over 5,000,000,000 paid admissions gave the industry a gross of $300,000,000 for the year, an average of 6 cents per admission.[1] Although the industry as a whole seems to have been backward in artistic achievement, the demand for film continued to be phenomenal. Sennett meant to see that Keystone cashed in on this demand, correctly sensing that it could only move in an upward direction.

In February, 1913, Keystone announced a policy of one full reel per week to accompany the two half-reels of 500-foot comedies that it was providing for Mutual release. This meant five comedies weekly to replace the two which Keystone had supplied just a little more than four months before. By June, 1913, the split-reel comedy was on its way out. An occasional release thereafter found a short comedy coupled with a short "educational" subject, but by and large, the full-reel comedy which was released three times weekly became the Keystone standard in the latter half of the year.

Such production held several important ramifications. Full-reel Keystones were rented to first-run houses for $20 daily. The antici-

[1] Henry Lanier in *The World's Work* (June, 1914).

pated return to Keystone on a $400 to $800 investment was in the neighborhood of $2,500 to $7,500.[2] With such a profit margin, Sennett was able to devote more time, money, and effort to his comedies in an attempt to raise their quality and appeal. He felt that this would be returned manyfold by an increased demand, proving himself to be a pretty good businessman in the process.

The year 1913 was an important year for Keystone. There was an increase in production and quality, and Sennett's salary rose to $250 weekly. Other things of equal importance happened to his merry little band. Fred Mace's popularity had become tremendous. In March, he bought 10,000 picture postcards of himself in a characteristic comic pose. The demands of his fans exhausted this supply within one month. Mace handed in his two-week notice at the end of the month and left Keystone on April 12. He had the idea that he could prosper on his own, a sad decision.[3]

Karl Coolidge threw up his hands in dismay and quit in May to get married and take a vacation. A methodical man to whom routine had a sound value, Coolidge had come to the realization that if he did not leave the Keystone madhouse, he would wind up in a real one shortly. As we will see, Sennett had little use for writers and was in the habit of making his gag men tell him the story so that he could visualize it. This in effect bypassed the scenario editor. Coolidge's resignation left Keystone without a script editor, a fact which bothered Sennett very little.

It did bother Kessel and Bauman, however, and the New York Motion Picture Company sent several men to Keystone in an effort to fill the vacant spot. Neither Kessel nor Bauman ever fully realized or appreciated Sennett's method of working, but they did

[2] These comedies earned between $15,000 and $25,000 at the box office, but under the terms of the agreement with Mutual, who paid 10 cents per release foot, the bulk of the income went to the releasing house. Kessel and Bauman often regretted signing that two-year agreement in April, 1913, but even so, Keystone netted more than $300,000 during the year 1913. Mutual's profit is a figure lost to history, but its gross on Keystone product alone during the year must have been over $2,000,000.

[3] Mace organized his own firm with release through Mutual. He began by exploiting the "One-Round O'Brien" character of Biograph days, but production mishaps closed him down soon afterwards. Moving to Apollo, he signed Bud Duncan (from the Kalem team of Ham and Bud), but this also failed to work out as anticipated. A third move saw the formation of the Fred Mace Feature Film Company—a third failure. He returned to Keystone in 1915 and left for good in 1916.

appreciate the financial return, and as a result, they did not bother him much during the year. It was not until Craig Hutchison arrived the following year that Keystone once again had a permanent story editor.[4]

Character actors came and left Keystone with a degree of regu-lartity. Dot Farley, who had joined the company shortly after its inception, quit in March to join the St. Louis Motion Picture Company, and Evelyn Quick left in May. Dave Lewis, a skilled racing driver, came to handle the careening automobiles that had become a way of life in the Keystone comedies. Emma Clifton joined the firm, as did George Nichols and Sennett's friend from Biograph days, Wilfred Lucas—both as directors. Keystone had three separate crews at work when a man who would become an all-time great applied for a job. He called himself Roscoe Arbuckle.

A native of Smith Center, Kansas, Arbuckle's background had been typical of the comics already on the payroll—stock, musical comedy, vaudeville, and unemployment. It was difficult to support 285 pounds when out of work, and Arbuckle needed a job. He had served a brief but unsuccessful apprenticeship with the Selig Poly-scope Company in 1909 and was now convinced that the movies were ready for him. Sennett put him into a Kop uniform, paid him five dollars a day, and let Roscoe go through three pictures.[5] For all of his bulk, Arbuckle was a surprisingly agile man, and in addition, he was funny.

Although Sennett was not too happy about Arbuckle's prospects as a potential Keystone comedian, Mabel Normand seems to have been the one who recognized his comic talent and persuaded Sen-nett to put the fat man in a leading role. The result was *Passions, He Had Three*, the first Keystone comedy starring "The Fat Boy." Within two weeks, Arbuckle and Normand were working together; Keystone Mabel and The Fat Boy were to become the most popular team Sennett ever had at Keystone.

Sennett had a knack for almost losing talent, or for not noticing it at all. At times, it rivaled his positive abilities. Although he was

---

[4] Whenever anyone from New York visited the Keystone lot during this interval, they found Reed Heustis behind the story editor's desk.

[5] Arbuckle seems to have made his first Keystone appearance in *The Gangsters*.

responsible for developing many stars, he let Harold Lloyd and several others slip through his fingers. He was unable to understand Chaplin, was not very impressed with Arbuckle at the outset, and paid no attention to Lloyd, who spent a few weeks on the lot in 1915. Hank Mann, Al St. John, and Chester Conklin gradually slipped away because of salary problems. In his autobiography, Sennett placed the blame on Kessel and Bauman for the low salaries which he paid in comparison with other companies. This was not exactly the truth. Sennett had been given the authority to run the lot as he saw fit, providing grosses held up accordingly. But any exhorbitant pay increases were subject to final approval by the home office.

Sennett paid whatever he could get away with paying, depending upon the particular individual. The lesser lights drew $2 per day, while stars such as Ford Sterling received $250 weekly. The only comic to come to Keystone at a good starting salary in 1913 was Charles Chaplin. He was hired away from the Karno Troupe for $150 weekly, and Sennett was so disappointed when Charlie appeared on the Keystone lot in late December that he mentally wrote his contract off as money poured down the drain.

Chaplin joined a choice group of comics. Mabel Normand, Roscoe Arbuckle, Ford Sterling, Minta Durfee,[6] Mack Swain, Chester Conklin, Harry McCoy, Hank Mann, Slim Summerville, Al St. John, Edgar Kennedy, Charles Murray, Alice Davenport, Phyllis Allen, Charles Parrott, and Virginia Kirtely all cavorted for the Keystone camera. In this competition, the unknown quantity of the English music hall comedian was about to be given the supreme test.

The story of Chaplin's year at Keystone is well known to all comedy fans. Lost at first in the madhouse shuffle that was Keystone and saddled with Henry Lehrman as his director, Chaplin was about to throw in the towel. He knew nothing of the business of

---

[6] In real life, Mrs. Roscoe Arbuckle. She had been the leading lady in a touring revue which Arbuckle joined as a tenor. They fell in love and were married in Long Beach, California, before he joined Keystone. Sennett put her on the payroll, and she became a long-time favorite of Keystone fans.

making films and could not understand why the scenes were not shot in proper sequence. Sennett's concept of cinematic comedy stipulated that a gag should be initiated and completed within twenty feet of film. Chaplin's idea of comedy was such that he was just beginning to become involved in a gag as the footage meter passed one hundred feet. Except for Mabel Normand, his fellow comics were dubious of his ability and held out little chance for his success. Even Charlie was unsure of himself.

It is interesting to note here that a leading fan magazine conducted a poll near the close of 1913. Its object was to determine the most popular screen players. Although no Keystone comic appeared anywhere on the final tabulation, most are better remembered today than the Lubin star who won, Romaine Fielding.

Financially, 1913 was an excellent year. Not all of the actual figures are available today, but they may yet be located one day. However, it is possible to reconstruct a reasonable approximation of Keystone business in 1913 by the use of existing data and interviews with many people who were associated with the company at that time. Mutual's initial order was usually for 50 prints of each film Keystone produced. These were for circulation in the Mutual exchanges. Since Mutual paid 10 cents per release foot, each full reel brought Keystone $100 per print, or $5,000 per order. Keystone turned out the equivalent of 105 full reels in 1913; thus, it sold Mutual about 5,250 prints. This meant a gross business in the neighborhood of $500,000.

On the other hand, Mutual could count on an average gross of $20,000 per full reel of film. Some did better, some did worse, but the exchanges could anticipate a gross of at least $2,000,-000 on 105 reels of Keystones. Since an exchange usually operated on 35 per cent of gross as expenses, it is reasonable to assume that Mutual stood to gain around $800,000 after their purchase of the prints and their circulation.

From Keystone's point of view, 1914 promised to be an even better year. The prints which Mutual had bought during 1913 would wear out long before they had played all of the theaters that wanted them, and reorders would be forthcoming from Mutual. More and more theaters were clamoring to use the Keystone comedies, and expansion was in the wind. Yes, 1914 promised to be an even better year.

# 6. *It Took Talent*

M ACK SENNETT had driven himself hard during Keystone's first year. He seemed to be the first one on the lot in the morning, and many of his associates would swear under oath that he never went home. As a result, the progress of Keystone under his guidance was amazing, but his personal life suffered. Although he and Mabel Normand had an understanding about their future, it was up to Sennett to make the next move, and at times, Mabel must have felt that her bashful swain was doing the hesitation waltz.

Social events to which the two had been invited often found Sennett in the editing room, putting the finishing touches on a film to be shipped east. Sennett hated dances, for his shuffle had not improved beyond the catastrophic stage which cost him the job in Raymond Hitchcock's musical play years before. The truth of the matter was very simple: the country rube from Quebec was unpolished and knew it. He also knew that regardless of how hard he tried, Mack Sennett would never fit into society. He might mingle, but he would never really belong.

For her part, Mabel delighted in the social world and spent a great deal of time both giving and attending parties. While they had been struggling at Biograph, the simple pleasures of a ferryboat ride or a walk had sufficed for her. Now it was different.

Money was no longer a problem. The future glowed with a rosy tint, and Mabel was ready to move up the ladder.

Sennett was not. Self-conscious and seemingly unable to acquire the luster of society, he found it increasingly difficult to talk to his girl. Sometimes it seemed as if they really had little more than Keystone in common. Sennett was in no hurry to marry, and, as is often the case with a country boy out of his environment, he did not realize that Mabel was. A somewhat moody girl, she was deeply in love with Sennett, and she became quite discouraged by the apparent indifference with which he often treated her.

Dates with other men did arouse Sennett's jealousy. He was especially upset when she went on the town with Henry Lehrman, but other than engaging in a few brawls (which did little to help his cause), he did nothing. Lehrman had a crush on Mabel, but he also enjoyed Sennett's discomfort. Picking a fight with her date seemed to be Sennett's only response, and occasionally Mabel would refuse to talk to him for several days after such a performance. It was a classic situation, only in reverse. Mabel ran hard to catch Mack, using all of her feminine wiles but wearing her heart on her sleeve. Mack ran hard in the opposite direction, to avoid being put on the spot. Gradually, the flame that had once been love diminished to a flicker of mutual admiration. Sennett was in the process of losing a valuable comic. He would soon succeed.

Business was booming as the year 1914 opened. Operating at full capacity, Keystone was producing the best-known and most-imitated comedies in the motion-picture world. Expansion was on everyone's mind. Late in 1913, Kessel and Bauman had decided on a new stage for shooting purposes, and a sixty- by eighty-foot addition had been completed. Mack Sennett had great plans for Keystone this year and talked his two partners into agreeing to additional studio space of seventy by one hundred feet.

The Keystone laboratory in downtown Los Angeles had been badly damaged by a fire in early March, and two printing machines were destroyed. Also ruined were the negatives of two pictures which had just been finished at the Broncho studio in Santa

There is *Dirty Work in a Laundry* (1915) as Ford Sterling prepares to mangle pretty Minta Durfee.

*Courtesy Academy of Motion Picture Arts and Sciences*

As you can see, it didn't pay to trifle with *Ambrose's Nasty Temper* (1915).

Monica. Bert Hunn had been working late at the lab when he smelled smoke and investigated. Had it not been for his discovery of the fire, the establishment would have burned to the ground, destroying many Keystone negatives and causing a halt in the release program.

This misfortune was another buffer to Sennett's argument that all facilities should be located on the lot, and in view of the loss, Adam Kessel agreed. The second addition was constructed and contained all the necessary props and other furnishings. Its size would easily allow eight to ten separate companies to function at one time. Keystone had acquired three additional directors: Robert Thornby, Rube Miller, and Charles Avery.[1] This had given Sennett seven active units at one time, a situation that had taxed the company's rather limited facilities to the utmost.

The year began with all sorts of problems. An unknown Englishman, Charles Chaplin, had joined the troupe and was complaining about Lehrman. Lehrman reacted with his characteristic brashness. He knew comedy and how to create laughter from celluloid images and resented Chaplin's inference that his directing was not right. When Sennett failed to exercise his authority and clamp down on the little comedian, Lehrman revolted. He and Thornby walked out.[2] They were not the first to leave Keystone employ in 1914.

Ford Sterling had been smarting for some time. His popularity had reached an all-time peak after Fred Mace departed. Sterling began writing, directing, and starring in his films, all for $250 weekly. By October, 1913, he had come to the conclusion that Sennett was getting the better part of the arrangement and decided

[1] Avery was promoted from the ranks in accordance with Sennett's theory that the best Keystone directors were those who had learned by starting at the bottom.

[2] In his autobiography, Chaplin stated that Lehrman had decided to leave Keystone before Charlie joined and was only working on the lot out of kindness to Sennett. This story depends upon the person telling it, for many of Sennett's associates deny Chaplin's version. According to them, Lehrman left Keystone because of a better offer from Ford Sterling—an offer that allowed him to tell Chaplin, Sennett, and Keystone to go fly a kite. Lehrman's ambition and personality lends greater credence to the latter story. His reputation within the industry was not one which included kindness, but all conceded that he was ingenious as a director and gag man.

73

to ask for more money. Salary raises of the size Sterling wanted ($500 weekly) were in the range of those approved only by the New York Motion Picture Company—in this case, Sennett's hands were tied. When Adam Kessel heard of his demand, he was appalled. Kessel and Bauman stalled the matter until after Chaplin had been signed, then offered Sterling another $100 weekly in lieu of his suggested increase.[3]

Sterling was hurt and dismayed. He had carried the company through the difficult days after Mace's departure, and in doing so, had proven himself to be the top comic on the lot. Now, the apparent lack of gratitude in return overwhelmed him. Sterling was not able to believe that Keystone would let him go that easily. He felt that such a long and profitable arrangement just could not die overnight. Sadly, that is exactly what happened.

Contrary to another legend, Chaplin's films were not the cause of Sterling's departure. Chaplin's first film was not released until February 2, and no one knew how the public would react to his portrayal in *Making a Living*. It was a good ten weeks after its release before his popularity became measurable to any degree. The story that Sterling knew he was finished at Keystone when he saw Chaplin's repertoire of comic tricks is nonsense. No comedian on the lot—least of all the Englishman himself—could have predicted the popularity that would soon descend upon Chaplin. As the most reliable judge of what would or would not prove popular, Sennett even admitted discouragement with Chaplin's efforts for several months.

To Sterling, it appeared that he was wasting his time and talents on an ungrateful management. Carl Laemmle had indirectly approached him back in October when rumors flew of Sterling's discontent. Laemmle's offer included a separate company of his own and a profit-sharing arrangement, plus salary. In addition, Universal would finance the new project. Sterling decided that Laem-

---

[3] Some historians give the credit for Chaplin's discovery to Kessel and Bauman; others give it to Sennett and Mabel Normand. Regardless of who first considered him as a possibility for Keystone, it was not realized that Chaplin's popularity would ever exceed that of any other comic on the lot.

mle's road was the brightest. Packing his bag, he said good-by and moved over to the Universal lot in early February, 1914. Lehrman and Thornby were invited to join him, and they quickly left Keystone. Fred Balshofer and Paul Jacobs went with them.

Paul Jacobs was a discovery of Lehrman. Early in 1913, he had need of a very small child for a comedy bit. The director found exactly the boy he wanted just a few yards from the studio. Young Paul was only three years old, but turned out to be a natural actor in front of the camera, and he reveled in the Keystone antics. Lehrman used him whenever a child role came along, working with the boy until he had the scene down perfect.

A bright child, little Paul learned fast and when Thornby joined the organization, Lehrman turned the boy over to him. Thornby had a natural way with children, and so the character of "Little Billy" was born. His first starring screen role was released in January, 1914, as *Little Billy's Triumph*. Three others had been finished when they all trouped over to the new Sterling brand. The "Little Billy" character was continued there and proved to be the staple release of a company doomed from its inception. Sterling had no idea of just how miserly Laemmle could be until it was too late. The Sterling comedies proved to be less popular than expected, and Laemmle quickly closed down tightly on the Universal purse strings. A wiser man would have profited by Mace's unfortunate experiences away from Keystone.

Ford had created the character of "Snookee" in his Sterling comedies, and Emma Clifton left Keystone to support him. The characterization was very similar to his Keystone roles, and Miss Clifton's portrayals were an attempt to imitate Mabel Normand. Neither was very successful, and Sterling took a vacation to marry Teddy Sampson.[4] She became his new costar, but this change did not shore up a failing program. Sterling's venture lasted only one year and as it closed, Ford offered to return to Keystone. Sennett gladly took him back into the fold and also placed his wife on the

---

[4] Miss Sampson had acted in pictures for various other Mutual affiliates prior to her marriage to Sterling.

payroll. Sterling had become another victim of one of Laemmle's talent-raiding forays.[5] These raids had captured a number of unfortunate victims. Unless the arrangement proved to be a profitable one at the very outset, Laemmle lost interest quickly.

Fortunately for Keystone, Sterling was hardly missed during the year. Chaplin helped to take up the slack and was soon rivaling Arbuckle in popularity. Mabel Normand was well received by Keystone fans and had turned down many attractive offers to leave Keystone.[6] Business was good and getting better. Theaters continued to spring up across the country, and as Sennett had foreseen, the demand for Keystone comedies continued to rise.

Mutual was now receiving $50 daily for first-run showings of the two-reelers, which were bringing in an average of $40,000 on their initial trip around the circuit. In an effort to make better films, costs had gone up to the point where $1,000 to $1,800 were expended every week. A few of the films were made at much less cost, for Sennett continued to use any event which promised to be an interesting background. When the industry held a Thanksgiving Ball at Venice in 1914, guests arrived to find a string of arc lamps and a Bell and Howell camera belonging to Keystone. The grand march was captured on film and put to use in a Keystone release.

Sennett negotiated for and received the sole rights to shoot moving pictures on the San Diego Exposition grounds, in return for setting up a demonstration of the production of movies. Mabel and Fatty worked the concession which opened on January 1, 1915; three weeks later, *Fatty and Mabel at the San Diego Exposition* appeared on the nation's screens. Later in that same year, the same thing was done at the World's Fair in San Francisco.

Certain of the Keystone comedies made in 1914 did a fabulous business at the box office. *Dough and Dynamite* was one of these. A two-reeler, it featured a baker's strike, with Charlie Chaplin and Chester Conklin as two waiters turned pastry cooks. For a Key-

5 The popular Augustus Carney left Essanay to make comedies for Universal and suffered much the same fate as Sterling.

6 When Lehrman left Sterling to form his own brand (L-KO) for Universal release, he tried to lure Mabel away from Keystone on the basis of friendship and an offer of $400 weekly. Determined that his former director and sometimes adversary would not have the last laugh, Sennett matched the offer and kept his prized comedienne.

stone, the film contained very few scenes, with the majority of action occurring in five of them. Throughout the picture Charlie and Chester were at odds with each other, as well as with the strikers, until it ended in an explosion which buried Charlie in dough and the others in the ruins of the oven.

This particular film was received with a great deal of enthusiasm by exhibitors and marked the real beginning of Chaplin's phenomenal popularity. It also grossed roughly $130,000 for Mutual in its first year of release. According to Chaplin, on any given evening that year, *Dough and Dynamite* could be found opening in at least seven first-run houses somewhere in the country. This kind of business done by one film made Kessel and Bauman realize that something had to be done about the contract with Mutual.

Keystone had grown so large that its founder was no longer able to oversee every facet of its operation. After running almost a one-man show for a year, Sennett was forced to cut back his direct participation. He seldom had time to take over a role now; his time was occupied with the planning of all pictures, supervision of some, assembly of the crews, and direction of rehearsals when they were used.

In the past, the entire sequence of action had been gone over with a cast and with a stenographer on hand to take notes. The stenographer wrote down all that happened and produced a script to go with the picture. Of course, the footage was already photographed when the script was completed, but this manner of operation lends credence to Sennett's claim that he seldom used a script. But now it was different. Keystone's size demanded organization, and organization meant scripts and shooting continuities. Keystone's scenario staff functioned as a funnel for the material needed to produce comedies on an organized basis.

Gag men came and left their best ideas before departing from the Keystone payroll. The writers were notoriously clever in avoiding work, at least on a formal schedule. They were, by and large, a hard-drinking crew who detested being held to a routine of any kind. Newcomers to the writing staff soon learned the ins and outs of life at the Fun Factory, as Keystone had become known. It was a constant battle of wits between the gag men and their boss. Story conferences were liable to take place at any time of day or night. It all depended on when they could all be gathered into one room at one time.

To avoid being caught short, the scenario department took all kinds of precautions. Sennett had a habit of walking up the stairs and into their quarters without making a sound. This happened only a few times before it was decided that Sennett needed to be taught a lesson. Bribing the carpenters to elevate the top step an inch higher than the rest, the writers had a built-in alarm system which worked fine for some time. Sennett spent several weeks wondering why his writers had apparently turned over a new leaf before he realized that his stumbling on the stairs was not really his fault but a clever warning device.

Other new comedy stars were being developed. Nearly every major Keystone comedian had a special characterization by which the public identified him. Arbuckle was "The Fat Boy," Chaplin had his "Tramp," and Charlie Murray played "Hogan." Mack Swain became "Ambrose" and Chester Conklin took the role of "Walrus" in their never-ending on-screen battles. Conklin also portrayed "Droppington," the fumbling troublemaker.

The freshest new comic to join the ranks in 1914 was Sydney Chaplin, Charlie's half-brother.[7] Syd arrived in November and went right to work. In contrast to the slow, methodical technique used by his younger brother, Syd seemed to possess a pure Keystone approach to screen comedy. His characterization of "Gussle" was a brash and breezy one, with strokes of broad pantomime. Syd was overshadowed by the more famous member of the family at an early date, and never did fully develop his talents. His best-remembered roles came in the twenties in a rather spasmodic screen career which had been interrupted while he personally attended to Charlie's interests.

Charlie's skyrocket had ignited after what appeared to be a

[7] In his autobiography, Chaplin claimed that Sydney was hired for $200 weekly. Even though Syd's name was Chaplin, it is questionable that Kessel and Bauman would have approved the signing of another unknown entity at that price, regardless of name or relationship.

burnout on the launch pad. His first comedy role, *Making a Living*, had been hailed by the trade papers for its bright new leading actor, even though they could not remember his name. Acclaimed as a fresh and original film, its acceptance by Kessel and Bauman was played down in Sennett's autobiography. According to Mack, the picture was considered to be a failure, and even Chaplin has gone on record as disliking it. Viewed today, it stands up as one of the better Keystones of the era, a credit to Lehrman's talent for direction.

As pointed out earlier, Chaplin and Lehrman had clashed on Chaplin's very first day on the lot.[8] Even when allowed to work out his own comedy routine and style, the overly sensitive little Englishman was to come up with films that bored Sennett, who seemed unable to appreciate their humor. The fact that Chaplin was taken into the American heart so effortlessly proved that while Sennett's judgment of what was funny usually worked well, it was not infallible.

[8] Chaplin had little use for Lehrman, as his autobiography makes clear. Lehrman was a vain man, but he also was a successful director. Chaplin was not the only actor in the business who disliked him. By the time L-KO was under way, Lehrman had been nicknamed "Mr. Suicide" by actors and especially by extras. Lehrman had little respect for human life, especially that of actors, as Chaplin pointed out. He would go to any length to obtain the desired effect or scene, regardless of the hazards to life or limb. Thus, his nickname and a reputation which actually caused extras to refuse work calls from L-KO.

# 7. *"Tillie's Punctured Romance"* *and Other Problems*

SENNETT had one idea that many felt to be foolish. He wanted to produce a feature-length comedy in five or six reels. D. W. Griffith was at work on a super-spectacle,[1] and Sennett did not want to be left behind his mentor. Nothing of such a magnitude had been attempted in the comedy field, and Sennett always liked to be first. Approaching Kessel and Bauman with his idea, he found his partners' attitude to be one of great skepticism. Why rock the boat when the sailing was so fine? "Good Lord," thought Adam Kessel, "Sennett means to throw $50,000 right out the window and we'll never see it again."

After talking it over, Kessel and Bauman agreed that the idea was preposterous and based their reply to Sennett on the fact that Keystone had no star of sufficient magnitude to carry such a film to a profit. Sennett was insistent and claimed that he could sign Marie Dressler at once and without any difficulty, provided they agreed. The two partners were still dubious, but felt it might be worth a try if Miss Dressler could be delivered. Besides, Sennett offered to place his one-third interest in Keystone on the line, an

---

1 Tentatively entitled "The Clansman," this film appeared on the nation's screens as *The Birth of a Nation.*

attitude which was always a clinching argument with the former gamblers. If a man was willing to invest his own money in such a proposition, he must be serious, or so their reasoning went.

Contacting the actress, Sennett found that she would be most happy to work for Keystone if a reasonable salary could be arranged. When they sat down to talk it over, Sennett explained what he had in mind. Miss Dressler decided that $2,500 weekly would be reasonable, providing her husband, James Dalton, could be brought into the arrangement. Eager to conclude the deal and then contact his partners for their approval, Sennett made a promise that soon came back to haunt him. He proposed that Dalton might be interested in handling the resulting picture on a roadshow basis, as a special representative for the Keystone Film Company. The proposition was agreed upon, and a formal contract was drawn up for the actress. It guaranteed Miss Dressler's salary for a minimum of twelve weeks, and the contract specifically reserved the right of Keystone to handle and exploit the picture in any way the company saw proper. This added to Marie's belief that James Dalton would be allowed to exploit the finished film.

The next step was a story, and Craig Hutchison, scenario editor, came up with the money-saving idea of adapting the story line of Miss Dressler's recent stage success, *Tillie's Nightmare*, to the screen. Hampton Del Ruth went to work at once. What to call it? Sennett seriously considered "She Was More Sinned Against than Necessary"; in fact, he insisted on this until his writers pointed out that it was a long and cumbersome title, whereas one which included the star's name would rightly be able to trade on her reputation. After much haggling, it became simply *Tillie's Punctured Romance*.

Elaborately and luxuriously staged for the time, the film was free swinging in all aspects. Filled with earthy humor and somewhat vulgar in places, *Tillie's Punctured Romance* was a farcical parody of the city slicker–country girl theme. Although rather static and stagelike at the outset, the film gradually became more cinematic in tone as it progressed. The picture, which is still available for exhibition today, was to become a complete success in

In the process of *Hushing the Scandal* (1915), Syd Chaplin prepares to deliver the *coup de grâce* to a dazed Chester Conklin.

*Courtesy Academy of Motion Picture Arts and Sciences*

Watching Phyllis Allen manhandle Syd Chaplin, Slim Summerville gets a glimpse of what marriage to Cecile Arnold might be like. A scene from *Gussle's Day of Rest* (1915).

all ways, vindicating Sennett's judgment. However, his problems with the film were not over. Actually, they had just begun.

Without any fanfare, Sennett and Thomas Ince packed their suitcases and left for New York on July 27. When this news leaked out, speculation was rampant over the reason for such a trip. It was no secret that the two directors were often at odds with the New York office. There were rumors to the effect that Sennett and Ince were about to withdraw and form their own company. As for the directors, they were not giving any hints either way.

Sennett's reason for making the trip was really quite simple. He held a screening of *Tillie's Punctured Romance* for Kessel and Bauman and asked the two how they proposed to market it. Everyone agreed that this presented somewhat of a problem. Although Kessel and Bauman had attempted to have their original agreement with Mutual altered, they had not been able to budge the corporate directors, and all product of the New York Motion Picture Company's affiliates was still delivered at a price of 10 cents per foot for release prints. As we have seen, this meant an average gross of $5,000 on an order of fifty prints from a single-reel subject.[2] Kessel and Bauman had hoped to readjust the purchase rate to one more favorable to their company, but their efforts had failed. They finally agreed between themselves that they would accept a readjustment of only 1 cent per foot, but this too was turned down by Mutual's directors, who understood a good proposition when it was in their favor. To put it mildly, relations were strained between the interested parties by the time Sennett arrived in New York City with *Tillie's Punctured Romance* under his arm.

Kessel and Bauman's problem was a simple one. If their feature comedy was to be sold to Mutual at the contract rate, each print would bring in only $529.80. Even if Mutual ordered fifty prints on its initial order, the gross would only be a mere $24,490. Since Marie Dressler's salary alone came to $35,000, Keystone

---

2 Since a print was good for 100 to 200 showings before dirt, wear, and breaks rendered it useless, reorders for worn-out prints often put Keystone's gross on an individual picture way over this figure. Even after Keystone joined Triangle, Mutual still had a demand for the older Keystones and resorted to duping release prints, for Triangle was not about to sell Mutual new copies of older films to be placed in competition with the Triangle product.

would have had to sell Mutual one hundred prints in order to break even on costs, or the entire project would become a financial loss. Clearly, the answer had to be outside the Mutual organization.

It so happened that an entrepreneur named Al Lichtman had recently left Famous Players to form the Alco Film Corporation with William Sievers, a St. Louis exhibitor. Alco was a forerunner of the idea expressed later in the establishment of the First National Exhibitors Circuit. Lichtman's method of operation was to sign up the leading theaters in key areas for big attractions. Each theater would run a feature for at least one week at advanced prices. To make it worth their effort, Alco promised the theaters that second-run houses would not get a chance to play the pictures for at least six months. To make his plan work, Lichtman needed quality pictures that would draw audiences, and he needed them quickly.

A call from Adam Kessel arranged a screening, and Lichtman was impressed with what he saw. Here was a film that would draw crowds. What was Kessel's price to place this comedy on the independent market? The bargaining figure was $150,000. Lichtman was staggered by this figure, and when he had sufficiently recovered, he left the Longacre Office Building seeking air and money. The air was free; the money came from Richard Rowland, James Steele, and James B. Clark, three other independents who bought into Alco.

Recovered from his shock and assured of financial backing, Lichtman went back to Kessel's office, and a meeting of minds agreed on $100,000. Lichtman was to have access to the master negative, but Alco was to pay for the release prints from its own coffers. Kessel and Bauman were elated, as was Sennett. The arrangement had put them into the black by about $50,000. But Alco's story had a sad ending. The firm was a victim of sticky fingers in the cashbox and died in bankruptcy and legal litigation a few months later.[3]

---

[3] Lichtman and other officers of Alco engaged in bitter diatribes that effectively paralyzed the newly formed distribution firm. Alco passed into receivership just four months after the day it was born, and Lichtman resigned, taking Sievers with him.

In one of the "overnight miracles" so common in the corporate world of motion picture politics, Alco sprang back to life. Harry J. Cohen replaced Lichtman, and Alco

When Marie Dressler heard of the sale to Alco, she was highly disturbed. After all, she had Sennett's verbal agreement that her husband would handle the exhibition for Keystone, and now Kessel and Bauman had sold the entire thing. A suit was filed by the actress in Superior Court to gain control of the picture and to prevent Keystone from carrying out its agreement with Alco. Her attorneys argued that Keystone could not convey the exhibition rights without her specific consent and that a state-right distribution would injure her budding film career.

Marie Dressler lost this suit, and was unable to get the decision reversed on two subsequent appeals. Justice Newberger of the New York Supreme Court ruled in favor of Keystone in March, 1915. He decided that not only was the contract ironclad, but Miss Dressler's interests were properly protected and the entire matter had been handled in a legally correct manner.

Marie Dressler had one other avenue of attack open to her. Keystone had been unable to pay her full salary, and in lieu of payment, presuaded their star to accept a small percentage of the profits. She filed suit for an accounting of the books, charging fraud and misconduct on the part of Keystone. It was her contention that Keystone had sold *Tillie's Punctured Romance* on a royalty basis but that this was unknown to anyone other than those who were parties to the sale. In August, 1915, Justice Alfred R. Page handed down a Supreme Court decision directing Keystone to provide an accounting within ten days. If Miss Dressler accepted the figures, the case would be closed, for Justice Page found no fraud or misconduct on the part of the defendant. If she should object to the figure, a referee was to be appointed. She accepted the judgment and the controversy was closed.

Even though he was not billed as the star, Charlie Chaplin received a bigger boost from the picture than did Marie Dressler. The picture is considered today to be a Chaplin film. Miss Dressler

took on the exclusive distribution for Archie and Edgar Selwyn's "All Star" films. A short time later, Alco went into bankruptcy.

Archie Selwyn and John D. Dunlop stood accused of manipulating the company stock for their own gains, and creditors received forty cents on the dollar. Thus ended Lichtman's dream. But *Tillie's Punctured Romance* had already been disposed of on the state-right market, and its circulation was not hampered by Alco's problems.

went on to make sequels to *Tillie's Punctured Romance* for other companies, but they were neither outstanding nor overly successful. On the other hand, every film company on the West Coast was now interested in talking to Chaplin. Sennett was forced to resort to numerous tricks to keep such representatives away from Charlie. The following events are clouded by conflicting stories. Sennett claimed that although Chaplin wanted more money, he would name no specific figure and refused an offer of $400 weekly plus half of Mack's interest in Keystone. Theodore Huff, in his definitive biography of Chaplin, mentioned a counterdemand on Chaplin's part of $750 weekly, a figure that the home office refused even to consider. In his autobiography, Chaplin detailed some imaginative salary offers and counterdemands, based on a sliding scale. The actual truth probably lies somewhere in this twilight zone of claims. But the end result was Chaplin's decision to leave Keystone. Imagine Kessel and Bauman's surprise when the news broke of Essanay's signing of their star comedian at $1,250 each and every week!

While in New York City in July, 1914, Sennett had been interviewed by reporters. They were interested in his opinion of the war in Europe and its probable effect on the American film industry. As with most other picture producers of the era, Sennett felt that the effect would be an eventual reduction of the foreign market to a zero point. During this time, all Keystone foreign sales had been handled by the Stanley Film Agency of London.[4] Rental fees to foreign exhibitors were 1 cent per foot, or $10 for each single reel. The foreign popularity of Keystone comedies was on a par with the rising domestic demand. Sennett's forecast of a falling market abroad never came to pass, and Keystone continued to earn a handsome figure from foreign demand.[5]

[4] Keystone rentals had previously been handled by Western Import, a creation of Harry and Ray Aitken. As a Mutual release in the United States, Keystone automatically went to Western Import until Roy Aitken returned to this country to participate in the financial end of *The Birth of a Nation* project. Stanley Film Agency then became in effect a sub-distributor for Western Import.

[5] The films distributed abroad also came back to haunt him at a later date. After Keystone took leave of Mutual, Kessel and Bauman refused to sell new prints of its Keystone negatives to replace the prints which had worn out in circulation. Mutual took to duping the better of the remaining release prints and finally resorted to foreign dupes of the Keystones sold overseas during this period. Neither Sennett nor Keystone ever received a cent from these illegal prints.

Sennett spent eight days in the East before leaving for California. Ince settled his business affairs, and the two men arrived back at work on August 11. In New York, Kessel and Bauman were still deeply embroiled in the divisions within the Mutual Film Corporation, whose directors were, among other things, peeved over the deal consummated with Alco. There had been no obligation on the part of Kessel and Bauman to market *Tillie's Punctured Romance* through Mutual; the corporation officers had just expected that it would be done this way.[6]

All the elements of a power struggle were building up within the organization, and Harry Aitken's authority was being challenged, although ever so slightly at the outset. Aitken stood accused by John R. Freuler and Samuel S. Hutchison (both of the American Film Company and directors of Mutual) of favoring the Reliance-Majestic, Griffith, and Ince features over their own. The argument revolved around Aitken's refusal as president of Mutual to release a production of American entitled *The Quest*. He had previously given them a difficult time on other pictures, claiming that they were not up to standard. Freuler and Hutchison were very strong in their feeling that Aitken had to go, and they were busy lining up support for just such a move at the next meeting of the board of directors. When the chips were down, Aitken would find that he had very few friends left to help bolster his shaky corporate throne.[7]

Continuously pressing for a readjustment of the Keystone contract, Adam Kessel was getting nowhere fast. Whenever he was able to distract another Mutual official from the simmering pot of corporation politics, Kessel received a "No" to his request. Unwittingly, Mutual was rapidly pushing the two men into another spot similar to their earlier disagreement with Universal. At that time, they had simply packed up and walked out. The present prob-

[6] The precedent was established in 1913 when *The Battle of Gettysburg* was released under special terms and bookings.

[7] Aitken's personality did not help his cause. An enthusiastic speculator whose temper was much too short, Aitken came into conflict with the stodgy and conservative Freuler over D. W. Griffith's *The Birth of a Nation* by committing Mutual to a $40,000 interest without first consulting Freuler. Charles J. Hite managed to smooth out this and other differences, but his untimely death brought Freuler and Aitken to blows.

lem was not one which could be answered that easily, but a new contract was due in 1915, and Kessel and Bauman decided to wait and see what happened. Of course, this did not preclude their looking the field over in the meantime. They might just come across something better.

At this same time, Mutual was not endearing itself to Kessel and Bauman in other ways. In the past, the advertising had been done by each individual company which furnished product. The cost was naturally absorbed by the producer, although Mutual made use of a rebate system which helped out. In November, 1914, Mutual took over the advertising program of all separate companies. A new department was organized under the direction of John W. Grey, who had been hired away from Universal. The only catch to this apparent convenience was in the fact that Mutual required the individual firms to continue paying a fee for their advertising. All monies went directly to Mutual, where Grey allocated it as he saw fit. As one might suspect, the bulk of advertising space was soon concentrated on the Mutual Masterpieces. Adam Kessel and Charles Bauman were not at all keen about supporting other pictures with their money and openly stated their dissatisfaction. Aitken and Freuler were too busy fighting each other, and as a result, Mutual paid no attention whatsoever. In an effort to keep peace among the producers, memos flowed forth from the upper echelons to the effect that the new advertising program was being constantly evaluated.

Sennett's personal relationship with Mabel Normand had not improved during 1914. He had continued to avoid any entangling alliance, preferring to court her with automobiles, flashy diamonds, and other expensive gifts. They were seen together often, but Mabel also continued to date others. Sennett did not seem to possess the ability to let his hair down and have a good time after working hours were over. His mind was not on the parties, dinners, or other gala affairs which they attended; it was usually on business.

Sennett was worried about costs. His phobia for small economies was well known by this time. He would willingly spend $10,000 to make a single gag work, but getting Mack to part with $12.50

In *Gussle's Backward Way* (1915), photographer Syd Chaplin demands a realistic pose from his subjects.

With *No One to Guide Him*, Syd Chaplin is really being worked over by Phyllis Allen, to the horror of the assembled onlookers.

to fill the swimming pool was another matter. He worried about keeping production sufficiently ahead of the release schedule to meet any emergencies. Without an enclosed studio for inclement-weather shooting, the ever-present release schedule often came close to eating up the reserve. Sunny California had its drawbacks, one of which was the rainy season and its accompanying fog. Ince's Broncho brand was fortunate. His people were able to take advantage of Sennett's facilities in Edendale when the fog closed in on Broncho's Santa Monica studio, but the Keystone crews had no such alternative. Keystone had to operate at a degree of efficiency which would provide enough pictures to cover the release program when bad weather halted production.

Keystone was still growing rapidly, and in Sennett's eyes, there was little time for foolishness. Expansion was in the air again, as Adam Kessel had left New York City on January 4, 1915, to re-evaluate the Keystone facilities. Accompanied by his personal secretary, Mary Kenny, Kessel made an inspection tour of the Sennett and Ince plants and sent memorandum after memorandum back to Bauman in New York. After completing his examination of the studios, Kessel conferred with Sennett for two days.

Out of this trip and the ensuing conferences came the decision to erect a $35,000 frame building which would house a 70- by 155-foot stage, complete with all of the necessary lighting equipment. This addition would help alleviate the pressure on the print reserve used to cover the rainy season. One end of the building was to house the Keystone automobiles, wagons, and miscellaneous vehicles. Kessel had held firm to his belief that other facilities should be provided before the indoor stage was constructed. When Sennett finally agreed to this, Kessel approved the entire project. Priorities were assigned, with another outdoor stage and a two-story players' building first on the preferred list. Construction began in January, 1915, on the players' building. This structure housed 75 dressing rooms, complete with showers, baths, and lounging rooms. The outdoor stage contained an artificial lake 20 by 40 feet in size. Lined with 8-inch concrete, it would serve many purposes in the Keystone comedies. Once these improvements had been completed at the end of March, Kessel gave the approval for the new indoor stage and took a vacation before leaving on May 7 for the return trip to New York and a showdown with Mutual.

Fred Palmer, the Keystone publicity expert and sometime scenario writer, immediately began beating the drum for Keystone. Palmer called a news conference and let it be known that with the new studio which would allow shooting regardless of weather, Keystone was now the undisputed world leader. It had the largest motion-picture plant devoted solely to comedy film production to be found anywhere in the world. Once the new stage under construction was put into use, Keystone could accommodate fifteen companies operating at one time and independently of each other.

By now, Keystone had nine active units at work. Ford Sterling had returned to the fold on a two-year-contract basis in February, 1915, and directed his own comedies. F. Richard Jones, Walter Wright, Dell Henderson, Charles Avery, Mabel Normand, Frank Griffin, Charles Parrott, and Roscoe Arbuckle directed the other companies. Rube Miller had joined the Kriterion, Nick Cogley left for Mutual in April, and Dave Kirkland went to L-KO the same month.

L-KO had become somewhat of a thorn in Keystone's side. In October, 1914, Lehrman had stalked out of Sterling's company in a huff and founded his own organization with release through Universal. Lehrman-Knockout Comedies went into production with four units under the direction of Lehrman, Rube Miller, George Nichols, and Harry Edwards. Three of these men had worked for Keystone and thus had a feeling for the Keystone brand of slapstick.

L-KO paid better salaries than Keystone and gradually managed to attract other Keystone personnel, including Hank Mann. One of the better-known L-KO comics was Billie Ritchie, whose background, mannerisms, and costume marked him as a Chaplin imitator. There is no question that the L-KO product was inferior, but the ability to imitate as closely as it did was the ability to nibble at Keystone popularity.

By the spring of 1915, fans across the land were in an uproar. Movie magazines were flooded with letters complaining about imitators of the Keystone technique and reaffirming their loyalty to the real thing. The letter writers were upset because, in the opinions of many, originality had all but disappeared from the comedy scene. Everyone was out to achieve a measure of success by imitations—poor ones, at that. Now that the opposition had begun to get the idea, it was time for a feint in the direction of a changing public taste.

# 8. Life at Keystone

K EYSTONE'S CAST LIST in May, 1915, was an impressive one. Almost all of the leading figures in screen comedy were working for Keystone: Mabel Normand, Roscoe Arbuckle, Charles Murray, Sydney Chaplin, Chester Conklin, Mack Swain, Minta Durfee, Harry Bernard, Edgar Kennedy, Harry McCoy, Phyllis Allen, Alice Davenport, Glen Cavender, Al St. John, Fritz Schade, Cecile Arnold, Charles Chase (*né* Parrott), Slim Summerville, and Dave Morris. A solid supporting cast was composed of many lesser-known comics.

Louise Fazenda joined Keystone from the Joker brand.[1] Polly Moran, a veteran of ten years on the vaudeville stage, appeared on the lot. Her rubber face and broad burlesque quickly won the hearts of Keystone fans, and within a few years, Polly would become as valuable to the Paramount-Sennett program as Mabel Normand was to Keystone. Harry P. Gribbon, the leading comic of the Gayety Company at the Morosco Theater, had signed a contract with Keystone in January, as had Billie Walsh, a Broadway cabaret comedian, and Harry "Dutch" Ward of burlesque fame.

[1] An eighteen-year-old native of Lafayette, Indiana, Miss Fazenda had worked in stock for a few months after graduation from high school and then entered pictures with the Universal affiliate. At Keystone, she was to develop a line of eccentric comedy portrayals that would make her a favorite with audiences.

Mae Busch arrived in March, 1915, when Hank Mann left for L-KO. Contracts were offered in May to Bert Clark, of the Clark and Hamilton team of Winter Garden fame, and to Hale Hamilton. Hamilton was known for his popular interpretation of the title role in *Get Rich Quick Wallingford* at the George M. Cohan Theater in New York City. Even Raymond Hitchcock, Sennett's old stage acquaintance, signed on the dotted line in May. He was to report after completing a picture for Lubin, and started work during July on the new fall releases that would be marketed by Triangle.

Hampton Del Ruth rose from a $40 a week writer to become story editor, replacing Craig Hutchison. Harry Wulze joined the staff as a scenario writer. Additional cameramen and other technicians were taken onto the payroll. To most people, this concentration of talent appeared to herald another expansion, but in view of Kessel and Bauman's strained relationship with the Mutual management, it looked strange to insiders. Those in a position to know realized that big things were ahead, even though the wind was blowing calmly at the time.

As 1915 opened, mayhem and madness continued to reign supreme at the Fun Factory. While on location at Mount Baldy with Syd Chaplin, Charles Avery scared the living daylights out of three tourists. These people had been taking in the scenic views and had stopped at the foot of a cliff to eat their picnic lunch. Imagine their horror when a loud scream pierced the mountain air! Looking up, they saw a body sailing over the cliff, to land with a sickening thud a few yards from their chosen spot of rest.

Hurrying to the mangled piece of humanity crumpled on the hard ground, they paused and turned ill. The broken body before them could not possibly have survived such a fall. While staring at the remains, one man noticed something peculiar. Approaching closer to the still form, he bent down to read a label, "THIS DUMMY BELONGS TO THE KEYSTONE FILM COMPANY. RETURN AND RECEIVE A REWARD." The badly shaken tourists trudged up the cliffside with the dummy and were treated to a royal time watching Syd Chaplin and the cast go through their paces.

Chester Conklin went sky high for Keystone in May. While

shooting segments of *The Cannon Ball* for June release, Chester was the victim of a premature explosion of gunpowder. The scene, which was to be staged in the new concrete tub, had been carefully arranged, and everything appeared to be under control. Chester played a powder factory's inspector of high explosives, a nitwit official who carelessly discarded lighted cigarettes and matches as he toured the plant.

Conklin was scheduled to go out of the concrete tub as the victim of an explosion which climaxed the film. A mistaken cue on the part of the man in charge of the explosives resulted in his firing the charge too early, catching all concerned off guard. Chester flew high into the air as the concrete tub was demolished, but he luckily escaped without injury.

Chester Conklin was one of the most dependable comics on the Keystone lot. His portrayals excited laughter by their sheer stupidity and weak-mindedness. Joining Keystone in 1913 after a number of seasons on the road as a circus clown, the country boy from Iowa soon became an accomplished screen comedian and an even better scene-stealer. Only Hank Mann could manage to get the drop on Chester.

Mann was the master scene thief on the lot. In one never-to-be-forgotten sequence, Chester played the role of a defendant in the witness chair, pleading his innocence and begging for his life. By all rights, the honors should have been his on sympathy alone, since Hank Mann was merely sitting in the jury box as one of the twelve jurors. But unknown to Chester, whose broad pantomime cried for mercy, Hank simply loosened his necktie and worked the knot up and down. When screened, the tableau of the expressionless face of Mann, accentuated by the huge brush moustache and the simulated hangman's noose, caused those who saw it to laugh until they cried. This skillful depredation by the subtle Hank Mann had lifted the entire picture from Chester, and is an example of the on-screen ad libbing that helped to elevate the Keystone comedies above their competition.

Mack Swain was another comic who could pilfer an entire film with just a few moments on screen. A native of Salt Lake City,

Swain was in his late thirties when he became a member of the Keystone troupe in 1913. As actor and manager of his own stock company, Swain had served the usual apprenticeship in vaudeville and musical comedy. Swain was one of the few Keystone comics who could really act, and he was thus able to carry a serious role successfully. A large man, Swain became fast friends with little Chester Conklin, and the two were destined to appear in many pictures together as Ambrose and Walrus. The other cast members laughed hysterically while watching these two attempt to purloin scene after scene from each other. Their actions on the set rivaled their on-screen antics in vulgar humor. Swain did not develop beyond the Ambrose characterization while at Keystone.[2] But several years later, when he was featured in *The Gold Rush* with Chaplin, Mack proved that he could be a sensitive artist as well as a slapstick comedian, and he prospered in many screen roles until his death in 1935.

Charles Murray was building a reputation with his Hogan roles, as well as with many other parts. Murray was a Maryland boy who had turned to serious drama on the stage at an early age. Entering the movies, Charlie went to work at Biograph, and after Sennett left in 1912 with his group, Murray became the only comic of note left on the lot. Working under Dell Henderson, he made a reputation, and when Henderson joined Keystone, Charlie went with him. Murray's stage training enabled him to do serious work, but he much preferred comedy.

Charlie's Keystone reputation grew slowly but steadily. During his days on the Keystone lot, Murray earned only $250 weekly, but during the early twenties, he would stand with Ben Turpin and Billy Bevan as one of the top comics in the Sennett studio. In later years, Murray fondly recalled that a day's work at Keystone really was not so bad. It was all in the way one viewed it. For Charlie, a

---

[2] Swain left Keystone to appear with Billy West in Bulls Eye Comedies, but the influenza epidemic of 1918 closed the company down. He was next signed to a contract by the Frohman Amusement Corporation for a series of "Poppy" comedies, which retained his "Ambrose" characterization. Released to the independent market, these films did nothing for his career, which went into an eclipse shortly after World War I ended. Theodore Huff stated that Swain was kept off the screen by a quarrel with a vindictive producer.

In one of his earliest Keystone appearances, Harry Gribbon ignores the sign ("No Spooning Allowed") behind him in *Mabel, Fatty and the Law* (1915).

Syd Chaplin, the Keystone Sid Caesar, in a prize moment from
*Gussle's Wayward Path* (1915).

typical day could include a couple of pies in the face, a seat on a hot stove, a fall from a high window into water, and a ride through thorns and bushes. For good measure, he might even be covered with paste and chased by an angry bulldog.

As a team, Fatty Arbuckle and Mabel Normand continued to win new friends with their brand of togetherness. One of their best films of 1915 was released as *That Little Band of Gold.* Although happily married to Mabel, Fatty was greatly irked by his mother-in-law. To teach Mabel a lesson, Fatty engaged in a flirtation with Ford Sterling's date while at the opera. The entire affair came out into the open when Ford called Mabel and convinced her to divorce Fatty. She did just that, but poor Fatty saw the error of his way and began to court Mabel again with such forcefulness that she succumbed to his new proposal of marriage. The film ended with one of the zaniest wedding ceremonies on celluloid.

This satire of the growing acceptance by Americans of divorce marked the beginning of a new Arbuckle—one who did not have to rely solely upon rough or crude slapstick for his laughs. *That Little Band of Gold* was filled with subtle changes of facial expression which indicated that Arbuckle had skillfully mastered the art of pantomime. Although his career possibilities were not foreseeable at this time, *That Little Band of Gold* made it apparent that he would go far beyond the elemental comedy of the Keystone variety.

The Keystone studio was always a lively place to work. Everyone loved to pull a gag on someone else, providing they could find someone foolish enough to fall for it. Until they learned their way around and knew what to expect, newcomers were most often the butt of many practical jokes. Sennett always enjoyed telling the story of a Ford generator which Conklin, Mann, Del Lord, and Richard Jones appropriated and wired to a toilet seat in the men's room. Victims ranged from Del Ruth through Charlie Chaplin.

Mabel Normand was also a great practical joker. When Nick Cogley complained because his stack of fan mail was so much smaller than the others, Mabel went to work. Pretty soon, Cogley's box was filled with mail. Mabel had clipped coupons and sent his name in reply to every advertisement which offered information about patent medicines. This joke continued to plague the poor man for almost three years.

Keystone possessed a friendly working atmosphere, and the comedians enjoyed giving their boss a hard time. Sennett's punishments ranged from a bucket of water above a door to almost being fried in his projection-room seat while watching a day's rushes. Slim Summerville and Bobby Dunn had devised a water bath for Hale Hamilton as he passed through a doorway. The joke misfired when Sennett stepped into pace beside Hamilton, who was walking in the direction of the rigged door. Hamilton unexpectedly turned left, and Sennett went through the doorway.

Joe Jackson was an inveterate joker, who worked almost exclusively with electricity. Whenever someone received an unexpected jolt of juice, Jackson was given credit as being the culprit, whether he deserved it or not.

The gag that hurt the most had to do with money, a subject dear to Sennett's heart. Things were fairly quiet on the lot one day, and Raymond Hitchcock announced that he was leaving early. Since it was payday, Sennett did not think twice when a distinguished-looking gentleman appeared in his office and asked for Mr. Hitchcock's pay envelope. He produced a note from the actor which authorized Sennett to comply with the request. Without paying very much attention, Sennett reached into his desk drawer and produced the pay envelope, which he handed to the stranger before turning his attention to other pressing matters.[3]

Soon after this, Hitchcock returned to the lot minus the make-up and in different clothes. Meeting Sennett outside of his office, the actor asked for his pay. A bewildered Sennett tried to explain that Hitchcock's friend had already picked up the check. Screaming at the top of his lungs, Hitchcock disavowed any knowledge of the note and demanded his pay. When Sennett hesitated, the actor asked loudly if the studio was in financial trouble and hinted that

---

[3] For a time, Sennett acted as paymaster and handed out the salary envelopes to his employees personally. This was done so that he could express his approval or disapproval of each person's work for the week. A grunt from Sennett accompanied by a pay envelope held a world of meaning for the recipient.

this was an attempt to save on money. By now, the conversation had attracted a number of people, and Sennett was placed in an embarrassing spot. He came across with another pay envelope. It was a full week before Hitchcock confessed his stunt, and then it became the joke of the studio. Hitchcock had conned $2,000 from the tightest Irishman in California.

Sennett appreciated a good practical gag and managed to enjoy himself at the comedian's expense. But even the best joke could backfire and often did. Such is the case of this clever story.[4] Shortly after Ben Turpin joined Keystone, Sennett and a group of his friends decided to invite the cross-eyed comedian to accompany them on a Saturday duck-hunting trip. Turpin was known to enjoy the sport and had become rather accomplished at it, despite his peculiar eyes. Sennett decided that Turpin should bag no ducks that day, and to make certain, he substituted sawdust for the shot in a box of shells. Distracting Turpin's attention, Sennett replaced Ben's shells with the reloaded ones.

When they arrived at the duck blinds, Ben was placed in one by himself while the others went off to another blind to shoot ducks and joke about Turpin's reaction. Ben fired shell after shell but no ducks fell from the sky. He was about at wits' end when another hunter appeared and poked his head into the blind to inquire how the hunting was. The little comedian told him and the stranger suggested that Ben try some of his shells, which contained a different shot than the ones Turpin supposed he was using.

Duck after duck now fell to Turpin's cross-eyed but unerring aim. Meanwhile, Sennett and the others had experienced no luck at all, and when they stopped by Turpin's blind on their way home, they were dumbfounded to discover that he had bagged the limit. Turpin did not mention the appearance of the other hunter to Sennett, and for weeks after, Mack could not understand what had gone wrong.

By July, 1915, Keystone had grown beyond all predictions. On June 14, all single-reel releases were discontinued, along with the semimonthly two-reelers. They were replaced by two-reelers

---

4 Which may be just that—a story. But Turpin's close acquaintances insist that it did happen as described here.

which were released twice weekly. From its beginning less than three years before, the release program had grown from 4,000 feet of finished footage per month to 16,000 feet. The eight split-reel comedies gave way to eight double-reel specials.

Three stages now existed for production purposes, and eight directors were working steadily. A studio manager was needed, and George W. Stout was brought in to take over the position. Keystone's problems increasingly concerned logistics, for 102 persons were on the payroll, and Sennett could devote even less time to taking an active part in the production of his beloved comedies. No longer did he find much time to step in front of a camera to enact a role. Sennett had never been so busy, nor had he worked so hard.

He finally managed to propose to Mabel Normand, and she set a date: July 4, 1915. While Sennett wanted a quick and quiet little wedding, Mabel held out for a traditional one—church, gown, and honeymoon. They quarreled and Mabel became ill. Actually, her illness was the result of more than Sennett's stubborn streak. Sennett had relied more and more on Mabel and Arbuckle after Charlie Chaplin left for Essanay. Mabel had accordingly worked extremely hard, reaching a point of near exhaustion when one incident ended her personal relationship with Sennett.

After the wedding date had been set, Mabel introduced Sennett to one of her girl friends from New York City. The lady in question was on the Coast for a vacation and had looked up Mabel. Word soon filtered back to the gifted comedienne that her soon-to-be husband was quietly squiring her friend around. Highly disturbed about the story, Mabel decided to pay her girl friend a surprise visit.

Mabel dropped into her friend's apartment one night on the pretext of a friendly visit and assured herself that all was well; the story was false. She decided not to confront her friend with the story and said good night. Leaving the building, she remembered that she had forgotten her pocketbook. Back into the building and up to the apartment went Mabel. No one answered the bell, nor was there any response to a knock on the door. Mabel quietly slipped open the door and stepped inside. The room was empty, but voices filtered out of the bedroom—voices that Mabel recognized as belonging to her girl friend and Mack Sennett. She left without investigating, brokenhearted at her discovery.

Other things had also upset Mabel Normand. For many months, she had been convinced that she was more important than any of the other comics on the lot. She felt that her talent needed a bigger showcase than the Keystone comedies could provide. Sennett had agreed with her, but Kessel and Bauman had to be considered. On such matters, they were still making the decisions, and the two were happy with the *status quo*. Besides, they had not yet resolved their troubles with Mutual, and were busy working on a new arrangement that could solve their problems. Thus, disappointment combined with a bad case of nerves, a weakened physical condition, and the discovery that Mack *was* playing around with her best friend left Mabel easy prey for pneumonia. Needless to say, the wedding plans had been discarded permanently.

Although they remained the best of professional friends, Mabel Normand could never bring herself to reconsider marrying Mack Sennett. When he found out that she was aware of his whereabouts that evening, Sennett apologized, but it did him no good. He bent over backward from this point on, trying to reinstate himself in her good graces, but it was futile. Mabel was a peculiar sort of person, highly conscious of her lack of a formal education. She was obsessed with books and surrounded herself with much of the finest literature in print. Whether she actually delved deeply or even read the books casually is not known, but her defensive nature was revealed to all who knew her. With Sennett, she could be perfectly at ease, since his education was no greater than hers. With other people, Mabel had to carry out an act—something that was not as easy for the little comedienne as it should have been. Whatever the value of a marriage with Sennett, the flame was dead.

Big news came from Keystone in June, 1915. All production was to be halted as of July 1. After the New York Motion Picture Company's contract with Mutual expired on September 1, Keystone would no longer release through Mutual. The Keystone reserve of unreleased pictures was sufficient to fulfill the remainder of the Mutual contract. Kessel and Bauman had suffered long enough. They wanted a way out; they had now found the answer.

Harry Aitken's troubles at Mutual had also been resolved. John Freuler had gained enough backing to displace Aitken as the president of Mutual at the May election of officers. Freuler consolidated his position at once by buying up the available Mutual stock. Now he could direct the organization to suit himself. Aitken was none too happy with this turn of events, but he had an ace up his sleeve that made him smile every time he thought of it. Conferences followed with Kessel and Bauman, who agreed in principle with his proposals. All that was needed was a working agreement, and to gain that, Aitken climbed aboard a train and headed west. He left the train at La Junta, Colorado, and waited; his briefcase contained unsigned contracts and banking agreements with Smithers and Company of New York City. Three men arrived in town on July 20. They met with Harry Aitken and closed an agreement. The Triangle Film Corporation was born.

This was actually the death of the fabled Keystone Film Company. Production would soon be resumed as Keystone-Triangle Comedies, but an era had ended. Subject matter of the new product would not change too greatly, but its treatment would be somewhat altered. Keystone had been a voice in the wilderness at the outset. It had held all manners and modes of living up for examination by the comic eye. This was no longer true. Gone was the boisterous approach to minority groups and the impetuous "mellerdramer." In its place appeared a more reasoned form of insanity. The techniques used were as frenzied and disorderly as before, but the end result was closer to the changing tastes of the public.

Those persons who had made "Keystone" a household word were fast disappearing from the audiences. They were being replaced by patrons with more moderate tastes, and the Keystone comedies of 1915 had already shown a marked improvement in story line and content. Actually, the Keystone comedy had been in a period of transition from its very inception in 1912, but the noticeable break with the past came with the formation of Triangle and with Sennett's first offering on the new release schedule.

# 9. Harry Aitken's Gamble

THE TRIANGLE FILM CORPORATION had a checkered career, for reasons which will be examined at length somewhat later. But at its inception, the idea behind this new organization commanded industry respect and attention. Triangle was capitalized as a $4,000,-000 organization with Aitken as its president.[1] D. W. Griffith, Thomas Ince, and Mack Sennett held the posts of vice-presidents in charge of production. Adam Kessel, Charles Bauman, and Charles Kessel served with Aitken as members of the official board. Henry McMahon, W. C. Toomey, and W. W. Powers were other prominent members of the executive staff.

What Triangle really represented was a merger of Aitken's product with that of Kessel and Bauman, all under one name. The three vice-presidents were given a salary plus stock in the new organization. Sennett's weekly salary was now in the thousand-dollar bracket. Each of the three men involved had signed contracts to produce for Triangle on a personal basis, but using the resources and backing of the parent company. This meant that Sennett worked directly for Aitken rather than for the New York Motion Picture Company.

[1] Although capitalized for this sum, Triangle and Aitken were heavily in debt to various Wall Street banking firms. This shaky foundation was a factor which helped to hasten the downfall of Triangle.

Ince had his own plant at Inceville, and Griffith was given the other lot which had belonged to the New York Motion Picture Company. It was renamed the Triangle–Fine Arts Studio. Although many additions had been made to the original Bison plant which Sennett had operated since 1912, the entire lot was badly in need of renovation. Among other things, all structures were of wood-frame construction and presented a fire hazard. Hollywood wits referred to the Keystone studio as "The Pig Sty." The entire arrangement had grown haphazardly and had not been maintained properly. It presented an appearance befitting its nickname.

September, 1915, found work beginning on a new $100,000 studio on the Edendale lot. All new buildings were of reinforced concrete, brick, or tile construction, and replaced the temporary structures of wood and plaster. The new studio was a long-awaited improvement and was large enough to accommodate twelve different companies working at one time. In such a case, each company had a maximum of four sets at its disposal. Facilities for building, painting, and storing the sets had been provided, and a large sign now announced that this was the home of MACK SENNETT COMEDIES.

Actually, it was still the home of Keystone, for in forming Triangle, Kessel and Bauman had retained the old established chain of command. Sennett received his salary from Triangle, but he still had a share in the Keystone Film Company which paid him one-third of Keystone's profits. Triangle had not merely supplanted Mutual. Instead of paying so much per foot for its release prints, Triangle took 35 per cent of the total gross receipts to cover distribution costs. The remaining 65 per cent of Keystone grosses went to the New York Motion Picture Company to cover costs and profits, a decided improvement over the previous releasing arrangement with Mutual.

Costs and profits were two important features of the new contract. As soon as production got into high gear, Sennett was to furnish Triangle with two double-reel comedies per week. These comedies were no longer shot off-the-cuff whenever a suitable occasion presented itself. Sennett was in the big leagues now; his

*A Rascal of Wolfish Ways* (1915) finds Mae Busch freeing a frightened Fritz Schade in one of those melodramatic scenes that Keystone fans so well recall.

Phyllis Allen finally has the goods on Roscoe Arbuckle in *Fickle Fatty's Fall* (1915).

position as the foremost comedy producer had been recognized by all, and his product had to reflect it.

Whereas the early days of Keystone had seen a full-reel comedy turned out for $1,000, Sennett was now spending an average of $20,000 per film.[2] Some of the stories might not appear any more complicated on screen, but casts were larger and better paid. There were more men behind the scenes to be paid, and wages were fairly good for the crafts. Carpenters received about $40 weekly, and top cameramen were paid a minimum of $250. Two-reel Keystones were earning an average $80,000, leaving the company with approximately $52,000 on each.

The scenario department under Hampton Del Ruth was enlarged and kept active. In the sixteen months preceding the formation of Triangle, Sennett claimed that only three comedy ideas had come to Keystone from outside the studio gate. Harry Williams, a well-known song writer, and Charles Reisner had been added during this time to Del Ruth's staff. Reisner soon became the fair-haired boy in the script department. He would spend his free time in the five-and-ten-cent stores looking for gag ideas, asking himself what could be done with the various items he found. Once he had a gag worked out, it was filed in a special cabinet under its proper heading—as kitchen gag, garage gag, lawn gag, party gag, etc. The list went on for pages, and Chuck guarded his file with extreme caution against forays by other writers anxious to make an impression on Sennett. Jean Schwartz was placed in charge of a new musical department, and Louis Gottschalk composed musical scores to accompany the comedies under the watchful eye of the musical director, William Furst. Furst was responsible for seeing that the music was completed and rehearsed prior to each film shipment east. Further expansion of the scenario department came in September, 1915, when Aaron Hoffman, Vincent Bryan, and William Jerome were added to the staff.

2 This figure included all pertinent overhead, from story through cast and production costs. The inexpensive Keystones of the 1912–14 period made use of just a few actors, a director, cameraman and were shot on location to avoid using sets. Salaries at the time were low enough to help hold the costs down but production reports show a rapid increase in costs during 1915–16.

A staff writer, William Campbell, had been promoted to director (over his objections) and headed one of the nine units at work. By March, 1916, fifteen full companies were busy turning out comedies. Glen Cavender had moved from acting to directing, and J. F. MacDonald, Victor Heerman, and Fred Fishback were new additions to the staff of directors. Even song writer Harry Williams left his desk in the scenario department to give the megaphone a try.

Charles Bauman made his first trip west to inspect the plant and facilities in October, 1915. He was followed by Adam Kessel and Harry Aitken the following February in a five-week vacation-tour of Keystone-Triangle. Satisfied with what they saw, the latter two executives returned east on April 1.

Triangle had zoomed off to an impressive beginning. Its initial program opened at the Knickerbocker Theater[3] in New York on September 23, 1915. Many of the leading lights in the production world attended this first showing. Everyone was there, or so it seemed. Daniel Frohman represented Famous Players, Joe Engel came from Metro, and Winfield Sheehan of the Fox Company was there. Otto H. Kuhn of the firm of Kuhn, Loeb and Company was among the prominent financiers present.[4] Other notables included Ignace Paderewski, Mr. and Mrs. William Randolph Hearst, and Irvin S. Cobb.

The guests were put in the proper mood for the occasion by a number of selected and comely young usherettes in a special Triangle costume, consisting of Triangle hats and dainty pantalettes edged with Triangle-embossed lace which hung below their short skirts. The lobby was freely decorated with the Triangle motif, and every opportunity was taken to impress this symbol into the minds of those present.

Sennett's contribution to the event was the first of many Keystone-Triangle comedies, *My Valet*, made in four reels. To make

---

[3] Triangle's grandiose plans envisioned a network of its own theaters as showcases for the Triangle product. The Knickerbocker was the first, leased by Triangle for $65,000 annually.

[4] Kuhn had every good reason to attend. He had helped arrange the financing for Mutual and served Triangle in the same capacity.

certain that it met his requirements for an initial offering, Sennett not only personally directed *My Valet* but also took a leading role. The story was taken from an old stage comedy, and in Sennett's hands became a travesty which rose above the usual run-of-the-mill "rough stuff" associated with Keystone. Raymond Hitchcock made his Keystone debut and stole the acting honors, but Mabel Normand in the role of the heroine came close to rivaling him. Fred Mace, as the villain, made himself despised by all and turned in another fine performance. In many ways, *My Valet* was to be typical Keystone-Triangle material, a logical and advanced extension from the Keystone of Mutual release.

As a result of this successful showing, theaters across the nation were invited to sign contracts for the Triangle product. Many had already indicated a desire to do so. Such a contract provided an entire program for the exhibitor, making it theoretically unnecessary for him to deal with any other firm. A house could run the Griffith-supervised feature and a Keystone for one-half of the week. The Ince feature was coupled with the other Keystone and used to fill out the remainder.

Within a short three months after the program began to function, Triangle claimed that 500 houses had signed contracts providing for an aggregate annual business of $6,400,000. Foreign business played a large share in this success, for the territories of Australia and New Zealand alone dumped $200,000 in the Triangle coffer. By April 1, 1916, Aitken was able to claim 1,500 theaters in the United States as contract clients of Triangle.

As soon as the corporation had been established, Aitken moved into Kessel and Bauman's offices in the Longacre Building. But this New York address was hardly befitting such a grandiose operation; a lease was negotiated in the fall of 1915 for a suite in the Brokaw Building, then under construction between 41st and 42nd Streets. The sum of $100,000 yearly guaranteed Triangle sole possession of the eleventh and twelfth floors, plus the use of the roof. Inside their quarters were located film vaults, projection rooms, and offices. There was even a completely equipped studio to be used for emergency filming. If additional footage, titles, etc., were

115

needed for the product when it reached the East, such could be provided on a moment's notice in the Brokaw Building studio. A fully equipped laboratory was also maintained to produce the release prints from master negatives as they arrived from California.

Roscoe Arbuckle took advantage of that studio. Early in 1916, he took a crew east to make comedies. As much as for any other reason, it was to be a change of scenery for Mabel Normand. Recovered from her bout with pneumonia, Mabel had gone back to work in the fall of 1915. Within a few days, she was in the hospital with a concussion. During the filming of a wedding scene with Arbuckle, she was struck in the head when the shower of rice and shoes was thrown. One of Arbuckle's brogans was included in the melee, and Mabel slumped to the floor unconscious.

Her recovery was slow. It was also complicated by her desire to leave the rough-and-tumble world of Keystone. Sennett had promised her that he would take the matter up with the management once more when he sent her east with Arbuckle's crew. Notwithstanding their personal disagreements, he still thought a great deal of his prized comedienne. Even though they were never to be as close again as they had been prior to his "indiscretion," Sennett still regarded Mabel as "his girl."

Roscoe Arbuckle spent five months in the New York studio and also made use of the one located in Fort Lee, New Jersey (which was still the property of the New York Motion Picture Company). While there, he "discovered" young Alice Lake and brought her west when he returned in July, 1916.[5]

Arbuckle had assumed a great deal of responsibility toward the end of his stay with Keystone. With a natural touch for comedy, he wrote, directed, and starred in many of the Keystones. His judgment was respected by Sennett, and Roscoe was given a freer hand than any other comic on the lot. He was allowed to do whatever he thought best, which usually made scads of money for the firm.

[5] Miss Lake was a Brooklyn girl who had appeared in an early Vitagraph picture (*Her Picture Idol*, 1912). She was to become a leading lady with Metro by 1920.

The rotund comedian spent one week just to shoot the kitchen scenes for *Fickle Fatty's Fall*. He used over 10,000 feet of film for that sequence. One scene called for him to flip a pancake over his shoulder and catch it behind his back. He started at 9:00 A.M. and performed the feat on the first rehearsal. Starting the cameras, the confident fat man set out to do it once more and complete the sequence. The cameras rolled all day, but it was not until 4:00 o'clock that afternoon that Roscoe was able to do it again correctly while the cameras were turning.

Mabel Normand was allowed to announce a new contract in April, 1916. Sennett had finally been successful in persuading Adam Kessel to establish the Mabel Normand Feature Film Company. The contract allowed Mabel the right to choose her own director, writer, and story. A four-acre studio was erected and equipped with all necessary facilities. Production responsibility was placed under the general supervision of Tom Ince, and her films were originally scheduled to be released as Kay-Bee specials. Kessel and Bauman later decided to release them on the state-right market in the hopes of exceeding the profits made previously with *Tillie's Punctured Romance.*

Mabel chose J. G. Hawks to write her first script, and the story was to be entitled *Mickey.* James Young was her choice as director, and she arrived in mid-May, 1916, to begin work. Betty Gray had been cast to take her place in the Arbuckle comedies. Sennett was quite taken aback at Mabel's appearance when he first saw the little comedienne after her return. The change of scenery had been of no avail; she was in a worsened condition, having brought a hacking cough back with her. Mabel appeared worn and drawn, and her friends all commented that the sparkle was missing from her eyes and voice.

Young did not prove satisfactory to Mabel and was replaced by F. Richard Jones, a director who would become an important fixture on the Sennett lot during the twenties. Production began in August, 1916, and continued for nearly eight months before the six-reel feature was completed. Accidents, financial problems, and the star's poor health all descended upon this venture.[6] When it was finally finished, the film was announced for the independent market through the New York Motion Picture Company, but this was done before Kessel and Bauman saw it. When it was finally screened for them, the executives howled in protest. This was no Sennett comedy; it lacked all of the distinguishing marks of a Keystone comedy or even of a *Tillie's Punctured Romance*. Instead, it turned out to be a simple and moving light comedy about the daughter of a Western prospector who went to New York, inherited a fortune, and was pursued by a smooth villain who lost out in the finale as "Mickey" emerged triumphant.

Kessel and Bauman hurriedly shelved the film as being unmarketable, and there it stayed until August, 1918. When finally released through Hiller and Wilk on the independent market, the film became an instant hit with audiences the world over. *Mickey* played for four years on its first release and became known to exhibitors across the country as "the mortgage lifter." Sennett once estimated that the film grossed $18,000,000 over the years that it was shown. Mabel Normand left the organization after the picture was completed to join Samuel Goldwyn on a five-year contract.

Sennett had many other problems during the first year of his association with Triangle. John A. Waldron appeared as studio manager and immediately assumed a large share of Sennett's worries. Sennett delegated a great deal of authority to Waldron and placed much faith and trust in his judgment. Many of the older comedians complained that the insertion of Waldron in the chain of command isolated them from the comradeship they had formerly enjoyed with their boss. Waldron proved to be a somewhat ruthless, but highly competent and efficient, addition to the executive staff.

New comics, many of whom had been recruited from the stage, were added to the payroll. Joe Jackson, Sam Bernard, and the great vaudeville team of Joe Weber and Lew Fields were among the early acquisitions lured by Triangle money.[7] So was Eddie Foy.

---

[6] Jones had some difficulty collecting part of his pay and withheld the last two reels until the matter was settled to his satisfaction.

[7] Sam Bernard and William Collier, Sr., each received $1,000 weekly; Weber and Fields were paid $3,500 weekly as a team.

The Keystone Kops in full regalia and hot on the trail. A catastrophe is bound to occur at any moment in *Love, Loot and Crash* (1915).

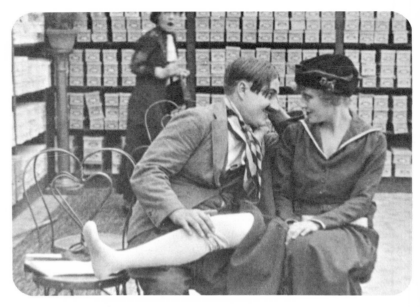

As a friendly shoe salesman, Syd Chaplin was one of the best. His personal attention soon became known as *A Lover's Lost Control* (1915).

Foy presented a problem typical of the stage-comics turned screen-comedians. He had signed a contract obligating himself and the Seven Little Foys to a year's stay at Keystone. For this bundle of talent, Sennett had agreed to pay Foy $1,200 per week. Eddie joined the company in the summer of 1915. After a number of delays, he finally set to work filming a part of the product necessary to get Keystone off to the flying start needed once Triangle opened the doors for business in October.

Foy was an individual—first, last, and always. He did not take kindly to direction by others and was fond of impressing everyone with the fact that he was the great Foy of stage fame. When things did not go as he wished on the set, Foy walked off in September, breaking his contract. Sennett did not say much, other than to ask Foy why he could not get along with Dell Henderson and the cast. Drawing himself up straight as a ramrod, Foy told Sennett off in no uncertain terms. He refused—absolutely refused—to be the recipient of a pie in the face. He felt that this was degrading to his status. Furthermore, he was not about to stand in front of a camera and allow a water hose to soak him down.

Foy felt that these demands, coupled with the fact that the gag called for him to be clothed in a nightgown, were near the height of absurdity. As he saw it, the absolute height was reserved for his last complaint. To add insult to injury, the comedy dealt with Limburger cheese, and Henderson had insisted that the real article be used on the set. Foy personally detested Limburger cheese and would have no part of such a maniacal existence as Keystone desired. He was through, done, finished. Telling Sennett to put that in his pipe and smoke it, Eddie then had the gall to demand a week's salary for the work he had refused to do. Sennett showed him to the door. As a result, his only Keystone comedy was *A Favorite Fool*, in which he played a tramp who married a widow (Polly Moran) only to discover that she already had seven children waiting to be supported.

Foy instituted a lawsuit against the Keystone Film Company and asked for $2,000, a sum large enough to cover his salary and transportation back to New York City for his entire family. The hearing was set for April 25, 1916, when Sennett's lawyers suddenly filed a cross complaint against Foy on three counts: (1) he refused to follow the instructions of his director; (2) he argued and wasted a great deal of time on set, delaying the production schedule; and (3) he kept an expensive company of actors and actresses waiting while he refused to work, costing Keystone an exorbitant sum for nothing. Faced with this counter legal action, Foy backed down, withdrew his suit, and left town.

Neither were Weber and Fields working out as expected, and they were still costing Keystone a small fortune weekly. The team had previously made a group of comedy features for the World Film Corporation. These features had not been very successful, but Weber and Fields knew what was expected of them in pictures and they did try. The two comics had the skill but lacked the basic desire to adapt to the Keystone technique. They knew that they could always return to vaudeville and probably command a higher salary, with the prestige of having worked for Keystone. As vaudeville comedians they were tops, but their Keystones were weak. Regardless of what Frank Griffin tried to do with Weber and Fields, most of the genuine humor and audience appeal in their films came from the supporting cast, which included Chester Conklin and Mack Swain, always dependable screen comedians.

Weber and Fields had more than their share of accidents in trying to keep up with the pace of life at the Fun Factory. The most serious one came in October, 1915, when they were nearly killed. According to the scene being filmed, the two were to be in a taxi as it collided with a racing car. Sennett loaned the unit his expensive Fiat to take the role of the racer, and rehearsals began. After the scene had been run through several times, Director Griffin decided to shoot.

The driver of the Fiat was supposed to barely miss the taxi but come close enough so that camera angle and editing could give the desired impression of an actual impact. During rehearsals, Griffin had urged the driver to come "closer, closer," and when he yelled "camera," things began to happen. To the two comedians sitting in the taxi, it must have appeared as if death was bearing down upon them. The Fiat came roaring down the road at 60 mph and instead of missing the taxi, struck it a glancing blow. The taxi overturned, throwing the comedians out. Its driver was knocked unconscious, and all three were taken at once to the studio hospital.

A delighted Griffin ran to the camera, which had been in the path of the oncoming Fiat. Leon Loeb had filmed the incident up to the last possible moment. As he saw the Fiat glance off the taxi and head his way, Loeb dove for cover. The Fiat plowed into the camera, demolishing all but its take-up magazine. When the film was processed, the entire sequence was preserved on celluloid and furnished patrons with many thrills.

It was sheer luck that had saved the entire sequence from becoming a tragedy, and the two badly shaken comedians wondered how much longer their luck could hold out. Keystone was not a movie lot; it was an asylum inhabited by madmen who tried to kill their comics and then shouted in glee as they saw rushes of the near-mayhem. Weber and Fields were covered with bumps and bruises acquired since joining Keystone. Surely, life upon the stage had never been this difficult or dangerous.

Since their comedies were not doing too well with exhibitors, Sennett was actually too happy for words when the two marched into his office a few months later and announced that they would like to be released from their contract. He gave them the release with his blessings; another load was gone from his shoulders.

To balance the ledger, it should be noted that one of the happy discoveries was the popular team of Joseph Belmont and Ora Carew. Belmont, who had made his stage debut in 1897, came to Keystone by way of Crystal. While with that organization, he had written, directed, and starred in the "Baldy" Belmont series, a name that carried over to his Keystone association. Miss Carew, a beautiful girl from Salt Lake City, had first appeared on the stage in 1900. Vaudeville, musical comedy, and stock followed before she entered movies with Goldwyn in 1915. She came to Keystone via the Triangle–Fine Arts studio. Under the direction of Walter Wright, the team was an immediate hit with fans.

As in previous years, other comics came and went with regularity. Hank Mann returned to the fold. Alice Lake and Fay Tincher joined the company. Juanita Hansen, fresh from her success in the American Film Company's serial, *Secret of the Submarine*, signed a contract in October, 1916, to work under the direction of Harry Williams. Anne Luther left in June to join Fox in a quest for dramatic roles. Fred Mace left for good in December[8] and Roscoe Arbuckle quit.

Arbuckle's announced departure was a big blow, as he had been the top attraction on the Sennett lot for some time. It seems that while he was in the East, Roscoe had let it be known that he was available and was contacted almost at once by representatives of Adolph Zukor. Paramount was about to announce a new program complete with its own comedies, and the organization was casting about for a name comedian to headline the schedule. When Arbuckle leaked the news that he felt ready to move on to bigger things, Paramount mounted a determined campaign to net him. Working through Joe Schenck, Zukor got Keystone's most valuable comedian. Arbuckle took Al St. John with him.

Schenck signed Arbuckle to a contract which was to become effective on January 1, 1917. He established the Comique Film Company, and Arbuckle was given complete freedom over stories, casts, and staging. He wrote, directed, and starred in a series of two-reelers that were to multiply by tenfold the popularity he had gained at Keystone. When Sennett heard that he had lost his most valuable property, he sighed, shrugged his shoulders, and wished Roscoe the best of luck. Arbuckle's move placed Sennett in a bad position since the newer comics on the lot had not worked out as expected.

Rumors raged around Hollywood in the spring of 1916. Harry Aitken had left Los Angeles on April 1, and almost immediately returned from New York City in Hollywood, where he was seen in the company of Jesse Lasky and Samuel Goldwyn almost every place he went. The three men even dined together nightly, which caused speculation of a merger between Triangle and Paramount.

---

[8] Mace planned to open another company of his own but died before it became a reality. He was thirty-eight years old. The stated cause of death was apoplexy, but rumors claim that he committed suicide with a dose of poison because of an unreturned love for Marguerite Marsh.

It was a known fact—at least to those within the industry—that Triangle was not faring as well as it might have been. It was also obvious to insiders that Harry Aitken was desperately attempting to connect the fortunes of Triangle with those of any stable and willing company.

In reality, the American Tobacco Company was attempting to buy out Zukor's interest in Paramount in order to promote a Paramount-Triangle merger.[9] This move failed and near the end of the year, Zukor was moving behind the scenes. He was about to mount a determined campaign to gobble up competition, and the privileged information acquired during the merger discussions convinced Zukor that Triangle was a good place to begin.

With the wisdom gained from hindsight, such a move on Zukor's part was somewhat foolish. Triangle was starting to gasp for breath at this point. The company seemed bent more on promotion than on production, and the various publicity barrages far outweighed the actual performance of the films it released. The company had acquired several theaters, such as the Knickerbocker in New York City where the first Triangle program had been shown to the public. Even with seats scaled up to $2.00, the initial programs had gone over well, but as time wore on the influx of stage stars whom Aitken had signed began to make less of a dent in their competition.

Some historians have concluded that Aitken was trying to duplicate Zukor's success by applying the same methods which the little Paramount czar had used to establish a foothold in the industry. This is conceivable, but Harry Aitken is dead and we can only speculate. Triangle was determined in its quest for well-known names from the legitimate theater to give the company a prestige that most motion-picture actors could not provide. But prestige does not necessarily make money, and Aitken failed to take stock of the fact that the market situation was not the same as it had been when Zukor made a similar move to buck the trust in 1912. Even Zukor had realized that the day of the legitimate-theater star as a

---

9 The American Tobacco Company had a rather large surplus of capital that was available for investment, and G. W. Hill, president of the firm, assigned Benjamin B. Hampton to inspect the possibilities of mixing tobacco and movies. Vitagraph was finally chosen, but serious consideration had been given to several other firms, including Paramount and Triangle.

drawing card had passed. The movies had created their own star-system by 1916, and fans were eager to see their movie stars whom they idolized rather than some stuffy name from the theater of art.

Although the Triangle features were luxuriously mounted and done on a fairly lavish scale, their popularity soon waned, and internecine warfare broke out between the New York office and the field operations. Aitken and Kessel and Bauman were soon at each other's throats, for the boys once again began to suspect that they were "being had." Under the extremely restrictive booking terms available to exhibitors, Keystone had ended up carrying the program along as best it could.

Mack Sennett arrived in New York City on July 11, 1916, to consult with his partners. The internal struggle was still below the surface, and the picture appeared serene for the moment. Underneath this calm exterior, bitter passions were being stoked for release at an appropriate time in the future. On this visit, Sennett was to get a taste of what it would be like when the exterior cracked. Ostensibly, his trip was the annual vacation-conference routine in which he had indulged every year since Keystone's founding. But Sennett wanted an expansion of the brand-new studio, in order to keep up with the demands being made on his production facilities. His proposal was to be argued and reargued before an agreement was finally achieved. One huge stage area, 250 by 125 feet in size, was to be constructed. The new stage, 45 feet high, would accommodate 75 sets at one time. There would be provided 300 complete sets, from which the directors could choose those needed for a particular picture.

The addition of these new facilities virtually made Keystone a self-contained city, on the order of Inceville or Universal City. The open-air stages covered an area of five acres. A cafeteria, planing mill and machine shop, plumbing and electrical shops, and a painters' area was provided. Parking lots, dressing rooms, a medical building, recreation hall, and office space were also provided within the boundaries of the lot. Over one thousand persons were employed in all capacities behind the studio gate. Keystone was the biggest comedy operation in the business.

# 10. The Triangle-Keystone Comedies

KEYSTONE had grown up in many ways. Not only had an increase taken place in terms of plant, facilities, and release product, but production itself had altered. Gone were the good old days when a director picked up a camera, 1,000 feet of film, and put his cast through their paces to turn out a 500-foot comedy in a matter of hours. The production system was much more sophisticated by 1916. Two-reel comedies were released twice each week at a cost of between $20,000 and $25,000 each. From 8,000 to 15,000 feet of raw stock were shot to be edited into an 1,800- to 2,000-foot subject. Crews ranged all over California on location and even ventured into the mountains far afield from home. *The Snow Cure* was done on location in Truckee, a favorite of Sennett's crews and over 500 miles from the studio. As many as fifteen companies were at work at one time to provide the footage necessary for what appeared to be an insatiable demand.

Consider one of Mack Swain's final comedies under the Keystone banner, *Safety First Ambrose*. The story had to be approved before it was assigned to a director. After the story department had spent four days writing the story specifically for Swain, it was turned over to Waldron and Sennett for approval. This granted, it was assigned to the director who worked best with Swain, Fred

127

Fishback. Whitey Sovern was given the job of assistant director, and requisitions were made for the necessary raw stock. For this one picture, 10,590 feet were eventually shot, a far cry from the early days. Fishback, Swain, and the cast went into production on October 31 and completed filming on November 27, 1916.

The final footage shot by J. R. Lockwood was sent to editing, where 7,755 feet were printed. The rest was deemed unnecessary. From this lengthy footage, 1,670 feet were selected as best representing the story line, and these sequences were edited together in a fairly tight manner. The picture, as completed by the cutters, was 1,925 feet long. This included 255 feet devoted to the main, end, and subtitles. It was shipped to the East on December 6, 37 days after the cameras had started turning. Release prints were made in New York for distribution through Triangle exchanges.

This was quite different from the early days of Keystone production, when everything had been done on a casual, matter-of-fact basis. It was indicative of the inevitable progress that had to be made as the firm grew. Such order was created out of chaos as a necessity, but it had been slow in coming. Sennett had attempted to cling to the "one-man supervisor" principle as long as it was humanly possible to do so. The establishment of a studio manager in 1915 was an indication of an end to the haphazard way of doing things. Gone forever were the good old days.

The Keystones made for Triangle release differed somewhat from the earlier ones released by Mutual. This was most evident in their content. They were still filled with earthy humor and were decidedly vulgar in places, but the pacing was not as fast, furious, and frantic as before.[1] There was an accompanying refinement in terms of casts and production values. Casts were larger and more effort was made in the direction of characterization. This was evident in the ordered madness of such films as *His Bitter Pill*, a gem of pure mockery.

When this Mack Swain comedy was made in 1916, the western

---

[1] Sennett standardized on filming the Triangle-Keystone Comedies for a projection speed of 14 frames per second, feeling this to be the best speed for proper tempo. Most theaters projected them at between 18 and 24 fps, which sped up the pace faster than intended.

was enjoying tremendous success. Foremost among the purveyors of western lore and action was, of course, William S. Hart. Bill Hart had become a national hero for his many portrayals of the "good–bad man"—the crooked cowpoke who was regenerated by love or sense of duty and walked a straight path ever after. When viewed today, *His Bitter Pill* seems to be a genuine western, with an added touch of sensitive, although devastating, satire. Swain played the heroic sheriff, but his role was seen through highly distorted glasses which over-emphasized and misdirected values. The extremely ridiculous subtitles added further to the satire.

Keystone made many other westerns on a lower level, such as *His Hereafter*, which poked fun at the contemporary western. This particular one featured Charlie Murray as a Hart-type sheriff whose problem was a gambling hall operated by Harry Booker. Murray's efforts to close the gambling hall did not advance the western film but certainly made comedy fans happy.

Whereas earlier Keystones had depended mainly upon farcical incidents strung together, most Keystones of Triangle vintage made greater use of a plot. For example, *Wife and Auto Trouble* found William Collier as a henpecked husband who played up to his secretary (Mae Busch) to the extent of buying her an automobile. His wife thought the car was to be hers, and Collier had his problems keeping wife from secretary until his sissified brother-in-law discovered the truth and the chase began. Such a plot does not sound earth-shaking on paper, but at least the story line *can* be summarized; some of the Keystones of 1912–13 defy any attempt at a logical and short synopsis.

The Keystone Kops had reached maturity, and in doing so, lost much of their early interest. No longer as ludicrous, the Kops now wore a different uniform. Gone was the "bobby" hat; it was replaced with a standard visor style by late 1914. Fewer and fewer Kops were graduated to the ranks of featured comics. The Keystone police force was still present, but no longer took a large hand in providing the fun. When their role in *Wife and Auto Trouble* is compared with *In the Clutches of a Gang*, the difference is most striking. Kops were no longer of prime importance in the ingredients that constituted the Keystone comedies. Sennett had moved far beyond the rather primitive approach with which he had started in 1912.

*The Great Vacuum Robbery* was unadulterated farce in the best of the old Keystone tradition. As two clever thieves, Edgar Kennedy and Louise Fazenda decided to literally clean out a bank. Crawling down a hot-air vent, they emptied the vault by using a vacuum cleaner and then left for a romp at a summer hotel. Stymied, the authorities called in a pair of "master" detectives—a return to the old sleuth formula. Charles Murray and his assistant Slim Summerville appeared as the bumbling detectives who donned female attire and trailed their suspects to their hide-out. From this point on, the film reverted to the pure Keystone format of years before.

Discovering that they had been located, Ed and Louise led their pursuers on a merry chase—into rooms, out of rooms, down halls, up stairs, through the skylight, and over rooftops until they were finally apprehended by the less-than-bright but lucky duo of detectives. It was a delightful tramp through the past for Keystone fans.

The trick photography which had been so well mastered at Keystone seldom showed to better advantage than in *Bucking Society*. Jack "Shorty" Hamilton was about to marry the fortune-hunting Louella Maxam. He sent an invitation to his old friend Chester Conklin, who caught the next freight car south for the wedding. On his way, Chester was thrown out of the boxcar. As he sailed through the air, Conklin's trouser seat caught on a mail crane and there he hung—suspended in mid-air but first in line for the next through freight. He arrived on time to wreck the ceremony, saving his friend from a fate worse than death and disposing of the female vamp in one fell stroke.

Production values in terms of larger and better-furnished sets were noticeable to the interested observer. This did not happen overnight, but seemed to be evolutionary, as if they were a Sennett response to the new taste in comedy. This new taste was on its way, but its effects were not to become apparent to most producers until

Vivian Edwards and Dora Rogers are impressed by the smooth-talking Hank Mann, but Mack Swain knows the truth about *A Modern Enoch Arden* (1916).

*Courtesy Academy of Motion Picture Arts and Sciences*

Disasters (natural or man-made) involving fire or water were prevalent in the early Keystones. At this point there's no use calling *The Plumber*; Charlie Murray has already given it the old college try. Looks as if the maid had better swim for her life (1914).

*Courtesy Wilfred J. Horwood*

about 1918. Audiences were in the process of change; the middle class was making its presence known at the box office. The idea that Sennett sensed this shift in the wind is pure speculation, but a backward look tells us that it *was* there. Sennett's success with Keystone had been based to a large degree on his wondrous ability to read the public mind. In view of his long, prosperous, and fruitful career, there is little reason to doubt that he was anticipating a change.

Action on the Keystone lot was maintained at a breakneck speed. The busiest person at the studio was Aileen Allen. She doubled for all of the leading comediennes in any sequence involving danger—quite different from the days when all had braved a broken limb, regardless of status.[2] A superb athlete who held records in nearly every form of athletic endeavor, Miss Allen's talents contributed greatly to the never-ending flow of comedies coming out of the Fun Factory. Directors often had to stand in line to utilize her services, a factor which tended to slow production at times.

Even with a super-stunt woman available, injuries were still suffered. During the filming of a fox-hunting scene at the Ortega Ranch[3] for Sterling's *The Hunt*, Dot Hagart managed to fracture both wrists in a fall from a horse. Since she was not playing a leading role, her injury did not hold up production, but merely served to point out that a certain risk was still inherent in filming a Keystone comedy.

Thrills were still as much a part of the Triangle-Keystones as they had been in the earlier Keystones. *The Village Vampire* told the story of an attempted robbery from a small-town mill and included Anna Luther's leap on horseback from a bridge into the swirling waters of a river below, Fred Mace's headaches when tied to a spinning flywheel, Earl Rodney's near-death in a stone-crushing machine, and the thieves crossing a deep ravine on a bucket line.

---

2 During the filming of one of the last Keystones for Mutual release, *Dirty Work in a Laundry*, Minta Durfee caught her wrist in a laundry mangle and was badly injured. She was laid up for months before recovering sufficiently to return to the mad world of Keystone.

3 A favorite location for Keystone cameras and only thirty miles from Los Angeles.

Sennett spent August and September in New York City, returning to Edendale on October 3, 1916. His head was still whirling from the ten weeks of arguing and bickering with Aitken and other top Triangle personnel. Sennett had gone to the city highly upset about the distribution method used by Triangle. Exhibitors who wanted to use his comedies could not book them unless they agreed to take the entire Triangle output. There were many houses across the nation which wanted to screen Keystones but could not afford this manner of booking. Such a restrictive booking procedure severely hampered the growth of Keystone. What Sennett wished to do was simple: open up bookings to any and all theaters, regardless of contracts. Aitken fought bitterly against any such compromise of his organization and held out for several weeks. In the meantime, the Triangle Film Corporation formed the Triangle Distributing Corporation, with William W. Hodkinson at its helm. How it happened was indicative of Triangle's rapidly deteriorating position as an industry force.

# 11. The End of Triangle-Keystone

Eₐᵣₗy ɪɴ Nᴏᴠᴇᴍʙᴇʀ, 1916, a new sales and distribution concern had been capitalized for $9,000,000. This new firm represented a combination of certain dissident Paramount interests under Hodkinson, a former president of Paramount, and the McClure Publications. McClure had established a motion-picture production company, and its distribution method was still unsettled when Hodkinson, representing the Progressive Motion Picture Corporation, approached Frederick L. Collins of McClure with his idea for Superpictures, Inc. Hodkinson became president of Superpictures, and Collins held the important post of treasurer.

At this same time, Triangle had attempted to resume a favorable trade position by offering to sell an interest in its twenty-two exchanges. Aitken anticipated that such a sale would bring into the organization ample cash with which to continue production. He felt that the pictures thus produced would restore the lost prestige of the year-old firm. Although the company had some of the best talents in the field of production at the time, Triangle pictures were no longer competitive, and the original idea of restrictive booking had held back its progress. Triangle theater interests had been the first to go; now the exchanges were viewed as an asset with which to gain more needed cash.

In late October, 1916, Aitken had proposed to sell a substantial interest in the Triangle exchanges to parties living within the territories serviced by each exchange. Even though it had been indicated that prospective purchasers should be thoroughly familiar with the motion-picture distribution business, the only real qualification necessary to buy into Triangle via the back door was enough cash to finance the proposition. No serious prospects appeared until after Superpictures had been formed. Hodkinson then approached Aitken and offered to buy all of the individual interests in one giant block for $600,000. This was a new twist to Aitken's original offer, but since it meant that Triangle would be able to liquidate its debts, Hodkinson's offer was one that Aitken could not afford to pass up. As a result, the Triangle Distributing Corporation was established to operate the twenty-two exchanges, and Hodkinson took over the reins on November 18 as president and general manager. The great days of Triangle were over; its remaining days were numbered; and its end was foreseeable to any interested observer. Hodkinson soon resigned,[1] leaving the field to Aitken, whose remarkable ability to survive upheavals can only be marveled at.

His financial stability temporarily assured, Aitken now turned his attention to other pressing problems. All across the nation, exhibitors were in a state of revolt against the industry technique of block-booking. This unique plan had been developed by Paramount, whose feature production had made it the industry leader. Under block-booking, exhibitors were required to sign a contract in advance for a specified number of films. These pictures were to be made within a certain time, and quality was promised by the producer. As a token of good faith, the exhibitor was also required to deposit an advance payment.

[1] Hodkinson was blamed for a lack of profit by his partner, Stephen A. Lynch. He and Raymond Pawley sold their interests to Lynch, who assumed the presidency of the Triangle Distributing Corporation and discovered almost immediately that Hodkinson had been telling the truth when he placed the blame for losses on the Triangle product. Lynch sold out at cost to Aitken and went into business with Sol Lesser. Lynch appears to have been the manipulator-par-excellence. Details of some of his exploits can be found in Gertrude Jobes' "Motion Picture Empire." Interestingly enough, a few prints of the Keystone-Triangles recently located bear a main title reading "S. A. Lynch Enterprises Presents." In some undetermined way, Lynch apparently figured in the reissue of a number of these subjects.

At the outset, this method had worked for the benefit of both producer and exhibitor. For the former, it allowed plans to be formulated on the basis of a certain market. Production schedules could be maintained, and investment risks were held to a minimum. For the latter, it meant freedom from worry about a steady supply of films. Rather than doing business with two or more exchanges, the exhibitor was able to rest assured that he would have a quality program and fewer problems.

Block-booking had helped to raise the standard of pictures by making names, stories, and production values the important selling points. The bigger the star, director, or author, the better the price that could be charged. Unfortunately, some producers misused this technique by charging more than agreed upon for a precontracted picture if the star's reputation caught fire in the meantime. This was done by labeling the picture a "special." Rental rates increased manyfold after this system had been in operation for a few years. Other such underhanded tactics were used to strengthen the block-booking system, and the exhibitors were becoming restless. They felt (and somewhat justifiably) that the producers were backing them against the wall.

Paramount, who had pioneered the technique, was also its most flagrant violator and thus the prime target of the angry exhibitors. Because of its weakened competitive position and Aitken's desire to undercut Zukor if possible, Triangle became the first major company to compromise with theaters by dropping the demand for an advance deposit. This decision was greeted with enthusiasm by the exhibitor organizations, who regarded it as a first victory in the long war ahead.

To return to Sennett and his tribulations with Triangle, the verbal battle continued for several weeks. Finally, he brought both Aitken and Hodkinson to terms. Shortly after his return to the studio, Sennett was able to announce that as of January 1, 1917, Triangle-Keystone comedies would be placed on the market on the basis of an unrestricted release to any and all exhibitors who desired them, regardless of any affiliation with Triangle. For all practical purposes, this announcement sounded the death knell for Triangle. Its most popular product was now to be made available to an open market; there was no longer any valid reason to contract for the entire Triangle program.

However, there was still a flicker of life in the dying body of Triangle. Coincident with Sennett's announcement came a report from Aitken that Keystone would soon return to producing single-reel comedies. When word of this decision reached Edendale, Sennett turned all shades of purple. He had tried to explain to the New York people that one-reelers were not economically feasible. Personally, he had no desire to return to the shorter comedies. His assembly line was geared to the double-reel product, and it functioned as perfectly as humanly possible. Why upset production now?

By this time, Kessel and Bauman had acquired more wealth than they had ever dreamed existed in their bookmaking days. Bauman was able to take it easy and do exactly as he wished. As for Kessel, he had bought a huge summer home at Douglass, New York, on Lake Champlain and a decent-sized boat to take him there. Much of the New York Motion Picture Company's business was transacted at the Lake Champlain location during the warm summer months. Both men were in a position of wealth, with advancing age creeping up, and their taste for battle had diminished considerably. Adam Kessel had suffered a nervous breakdown in December, 1916, and his recovery was slow. Yet, there was one good fight left within the two and they made the most of it.

Samuel Rork had taken over Keystone publicity direction when Fred Palmer left to join the scenario staff at Universal. It was Rork's job to let the world know that Keystone would soon place a number of comedies on the state-right market. This was Kessel and Bauman's reply to the Aitken announcement of single-reel comedies. Exhibitors were notified that they could obtain further information from the Longacre Building. (The New York Motion Picture Company had left the Triangle suite in the Brokaw Building to return home.) When Aitken heard of the state-right booking offer, angry statements began to fly in all directions. By his think-

One of Keystone's most dependable fun-makers, Chester Conklin, just can't stay out of trouble in *Droppington's Family Tree* (1915).

*Courtesy Academy of Motion Picture Arts and Sciences*

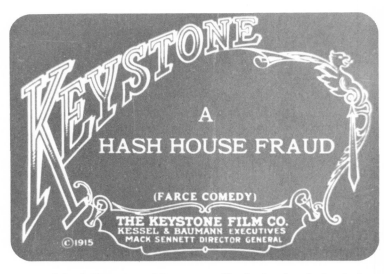

The original Keystone titles were effectively simple in design. Notice how "Keystone," by its size and placement, dominates the screen.

This title frame, taken from a W. H. Productions Company reissue, lists both old and new titles. Notice the prominence of Sennett's name, and the offset "Keystone," which had a three-dimensional effect on the screen. It carried a copyright notice dated 1918, but no such copyright appears in the Library of Congress' compilation. The notice may have been an attempt to deter further copying by others.

ing, this was directly in conflict with the Triangle-Keystone contract, and any such open revolt must be nipped in the bud.

After weeks of arguments, conferences, and bitter recriminations, a compromise was hammered out between the dissident parties in February, 1917. Keystone would not release anything on the state-right market, and Aitken withdrew his statement about the single-reel comedies. Kessel and Bauman sold the New York Motion Picture Company to Triangle.[2] Bauman then disposed of his stock in the parent company and retired. Kessel stayed on to form an executive committee of the Triangle board of directors with Aitken and C. M. Parker. McClure Pictures, Inc. contributed its series of five-reel pictures depicting "The Seven Deadly Sins," of which *Envy* was the first. Richard Ridgely had just completed its filming at the Edison studio. Triangle also bought Majestic and Reliance from Aitken.

Sennett was in a most precarious position during this period of negotiation. He still harbored a deep resentment of Harry Aitken which stemmed from Triangle's failure to join Paramount. To Sennett, the merger would have meant a great deal in terms of an expanded distribution of his product—a factor which could only have meant more money and prestige. For the boy from Quebec, both were quite important and worth-while considerations. Having bought out Kessel and Bauman, Triangle held the contract rights to the name "Mack Sennett" in addition to owning the Keystone trade-mark. From listening to the various interests argue with each other, Sennett soon realized that he held very little high ground from which to bargain.

The comedy producer knew that he would be fortunate if he managed to salvage anything, but the right to use his own name was his uppermost desire. He had worked very hard for years to establish his reputation, and now both "Sennett" and "Keystone" had marquee value beyond calculation. Carefully laying his plans, Sennett sat and listened to the pros and cons of the preliminary

2 At this time, Aitken was deep in troubled financial water. Triangle's creditors were pressing for payment, and although Aitken had constructed a formidable production organization, it teetered on the brink of disaster throughout late 1916 and 1917.

discussions. Without even mentioning it to his attorney, Sennett decided on a plan of action. He would put up a fight, but not for his own name. Instead, he would make a play for the trade-mark.

After many meetings, it became apparent that no reconciliation was possible. Finally, Sennett jumped out of his chair, screaming. His action took everyone off guard; no one in the room realized that the Keystone name had meant so much to Sennett. Their surprise was exactly what he had expected, and he took full advantage of the situation. Shouting about all of the hard work he had put into making Keystone a household word, Sennett skillfully worked his audience over before they retired in closed session to consider his demands. When the doors opened again, the directors gave Sennett their introductory concession—he was allowed to retain the contracts of all his actors and directors.

Sennett burst into another feigned rage and tirade, accusing them of evading the main issue at hand—Keystone and the title to its use. To avoid facing up to the possible loss of what they considered to be a valuable property, the directors countered with an additional offer. They decided to buy Sennett's stock in Triangle at the current market value,[3] offering to throw in an additional $180,000 as a cash bonus.

Caught off guard at the offer, Sennett simply stared in openmouthed amazement at his adversaries. This was misinterpreted as a move of hesitation, and the directors announced that they would not only include the title to the Edendale studio but would also throw in his name. All these things were his, but the adamant directors refused to part with the Keystone trade-mark.

Sennett found it hard to believe that such a stroke of good fortune had happened to him. At the outset of the discussions, Triangle had held all of the cards—Sennett had been at the mercy of its directors. Whatever they chose to do, he would have had to abide by the decision. That his attempt to salvage the Keystone trade-mark would bring him the studio, its contracts, and the fortunate sale of his Triangle stock was more than he had ever dreamed possible—

---

[3] Triangle stock, which had once sold for as high as $9.00 a share, was difficult to dispose of at this time. Sennett was fortunate to realize anything, but the bonus offset the loss he would have otherwise incurred.

and all without his lifting a finger. Sennett knew something that the directors of Triangle could never have been convinced of at the time: the name "Keystone" would mean nothing without Sennett.[4] Again, time would prove him to be entirely correct. In the meantime, Lady Luck had certainly smiled on her Irish charge.

Quickly regaining his composure, Mack left the Triangle meeting and hurried to the nearest Western Union office, where he breathed deeply and collected his thoughts. They were expressed in the following night letter, sent collect to his studio manager:

NEW YORK CITY, June 25, 1917

MR. J. A. WALDRON

Have just closed deal selling my interest in Keystone retaining studio and entire property and certain number of people list of whom will reach you by mail Tuesday or Wednesday. Mr. Patterson representing H. O. Davis will report at studio Tuesday to take charge of finishing productions now under way and will possibly put all companies in production immediately provided they can finish by July 15th. Co-operate with him to the fullest extent until my return in ten days or two weeks when I have agreed to lend what assistance I can to complete productions then in progress. Show this wire to Del Ruth and have it understood Mr. Patterson's decisions are final in all matters. Mr. Davis and I are very friendly so arrange to show Mr. Patterson every courtesy and consideration as Davis' representative. Discontinue further production on Woodley special. O. K. let Culver City use wind machine. O'Sullivan suggests stretching Morris' one reel Western Story into two reels. Take this up with Patterson. Dismiss Robert Kerr.

MACK SENNETT

The effect on Keystone was simple. As of October 1, the Keystone comedies were dead. Production was to be halted in July,

---

4 This was a point well made and recognized by the editorial writers of *The Moving Picture World* in their issue of April 5, 1919, when they said: " . . . If a few twelve-months ago you had asked a body of film men to state offhand the market value of the brand name of Keystone, would any one of them have raised violent objections had a member of the party set the price at a million dollars? Yet this remarkably valuable screen asset fades into nothingness so silently that the average picture-goer is unaware of its passing. In the minds of the screen's public, Keystone represented an individual. Take from behind the brand the person who is credited with creating it and the larger part of its importance is dissipated. In the film business, brand names are valuable as property if and when they represent an institution and not an individual."

1917, since a sufficient number of pictures would be finished by that time to carry the release schedule through the contract-expiration date. Triangle's claim to the trade-mark had allowed the company to establish several units to make comedies in both one- and two-reel lengths. The single reels were called Keystone comedies, and the double reels were referred to as Triangle comedies.[5]

A large number of the minor players, directors, and other personnel were released from contract by Sennett and stayed with Triangle to work in these comedies under the general supervision of H. O. Davis.[6] The style and quality dropped considerably, and a puzzled public began to ask, "What has happened to the good old-fashioned Keystones we used to see?" The imitations did not begin to compare with their namesakes and therefore did not last even as long as the highly imitative L-KO comedies had. Today, however, Sennett is often given credit (or blame) for *all* Triangle comedies.[7]

Keystone was now dead in fact, if not in name. The *coup de grâce*, which would come with the dissolution of Triangle, followed shortly.[8] Sennett took a vacation and went fishing; he landed a contract with Paramount. Zukor was only too pleased to announce that Mack Sennett, the foremost comedy producer in all the world, was now affiliated with him. The King of Comedy was to

[5] Triangle had previously made a series of Fine-Art comedies on the Griffith lot starring Fay Tincher, De Wolf Hopper, Shorty Hamilton, and others. Eddie Dillon had directed and made use of many of the minor Keystone players in supporting roles. These comedies shared the release schedule with the Sennett films.

[6] Davis complained that Triangle was not progressive enough and thus hampered his creative ability. Aitken, who had once considered Freuler as too conservative, now viewed Davis as too radical and let him go. Beset by financial problems as he watched his carefully constructed organization crumble, Aitken wished to have his cake and eat it too. The films which Davis made were low budget and low quality; Aitken wanted lavish films.

[7] Over one hundred single- and double-reel comedies, for which Sennett had no responsibility, were made and released by Triangle. Beginning in January, 1917, the imitations shared the bill with the genuine article. Mack's organization furnished the necessary personnel, and his less capable directors turned out comedies on the order of *A Dark Room Secret*. Directed by Henry Kernan, this single reel starred Harry Depp, Lillian Biron, Ben Horning, Elizabeth DeWitt, Lloyd Bacon, and Marie Manley.

[8] Triangle moved to making pictures "to order," a plan which failed to revitalize the ailing company. Aitken then reorganized it as a small studio and leased part of the facilities. Triangle's end came when its stockholders took Aitken to court to answer a charge of diverting company funds. His sole defense was, "I do not remember." This lapse of memory cost him $1,375,000, and Triangle went into involuntary bankruptcy. For all practical purposes, Aitken was finished in the industry.

produce comedies for Paramount release, one double reel every second week beginning September 30, 1917. Sennett had retained his executive staff and those players and directors he felt valuable. A slight reorganization, a new incorporation for $3,000,000, and Mack Sennett comedies were ready to flow once more.

# 12. *The Last Year-Bathing Beauties and Comedians*

THE SUCCESS which Keystone had brought into the life of Mack Sennett also brought him a good deal of loneliness. In the beginning, he had been just one of the gang—another member of the crew. His screen appearances had enabled him to keep this relationship, but as the production of comedies expanded, he found that the time he could devote to such activities became more and more limited. Sennett also found himself less able to fraternize with his actors; his new executive duties demanded that he adopt a sense of dignity.

A patriarchal attitude toward his players began to evolve from the administration building which Sennett had talked Adam Kessel into constructing. This two-story building had a gymnasium on its roof and included a tall tower which housed Sennett's office. From this vantage point overlooking the lot, Sennett was able to keep a closer eye on what took place. He developed a tendency toward suspicion of certain persons—persons whom he felt were lagging behind on their jobs. The tower office reinforced this feeling, for Sennett was a person who felt that nothing was being accomplished unless the activity below appeared meaningful to him.

By this time, Sennett had become known as "The Old Man," a reflection of his changed relationship with his employees. As with any employer, he had his individual quirks. Lenient in some ways, Sennett was a ruthless disciplinarian in others. It all depended upon how he was handled and how much he had had to drink. No liquor was allowed on the lot, except in Sennett's office and Joe Jackson's dressing room. Of all the comics, only Jackson had official permission to indulge during working hours.

Sennett's acquaintances noted that if he had put away a drink or two, he was more relaxed and less liable to procrastinate. As Chester Conklin told it, "When Mack was feeling himself, he was a darn good fellow, but otherwise, he could be real rough." Procrastination seemed to be very much a way of life with him. Actually, it was not really a desire to delay a decision, but rather to think it over thoroughly. Sennett was a slow, methodical thinker who often covered his face with his hands for several minutes at a time as he mulled over a situation. At other times, his face would draw up into what appeared to be a deep scowl as he thought about problems. He acquired a habit of doing this, and those who did not know the producer often fell into the error of thinking that he was really angry with them. Both of these habits seemed to work to his advantage. Since Sennett usually thought on a problem for days, it was seldom possible to tell by looking at the man whether he was actually thinking or really was mad.

Sennett's loneliness was well known and expressed itself in various ways, often to be mistaken for shrewd business acumen by those with whom he was dealing. When the new studio was completed and the indoor lighting had been installed, Sennett called Mack Swain out of bed in the middle of the night to come over and make a series of photographic tests. Swain mistakenly interpreted the call as an indication that he had been singled out to comfort his boss. Actually, the truth of the matter was much more obvious. Of all the comics, he lived closest to the lot, and as Sennett was determined to put the studio into operation the following day, Swain was the logical one to be summoned. Personal loneliness had nothing to do with business.

Sennett possessed an uncanny motion-picture sense. It matched his business sense. He thought in terms of photographic action, a

The Keystone Fire Department is not as well remembered as the famed Kops, but it was equally inept, as seen in *Bath Tub Perils* (1916).

Having won the lady fair, Tom Kennedy tells Mack Swain where
to go in *Ambrose's Rapid Rise*.

most remarkable consideration when combined with his taste in humor. This is perhaps the major reason why the early Keystones could be made in an informal manner without a script. He always held that a story that was too complicated to stick in a writer's memory was not suited for his purposes. He also believed that a business deal which could not be explained clearly and quickly was not really a business deal; it was a fleecing designed for the unwary.

With his habit of looking the situation over carefully before he leaped, Sennett did not like to be argued with or contradicted by his staff. However, "yes men" did not last on the lot very long. The ones who stayed were the ones who learned that he could be easily swayed, provided that it was cleverly done. If a director had a new slant, an indirect approach was best, especially if that approach gave Sennett the feeling that the idea was his own.

As mentioned earlier, his running battles with the writers were a good example of how he could be handled. Sennett did not trust any of them, and he made certain that they knew it. Periodically, he would arrive at the studio at 6:00 A.M. and stand in the guard shack at the gate. There he inspected everyone who entered and checked on the condition of his gag men. They tried hard to find out in advance when such an inspection would take place, but most often they met with failure.

When he first began building up the writing staff, all writers were placed in one bungalow without the presence of phones, newspapers, books, or any other distracting items. Sennett soon found it too difficult to keep track of the gag men in this location. They were moved into the tower when it was finally completed. Sennett also operated on the theory that writers worked best on an empty stomach; he lectured each one on the merits of a light lunch. This came about immediately after he discovered that it had become a daily routine to eat lunch and then sleep half the afternoon away.

When the writers left at the end of the day, they had to pass by Sennett's office on the way out. His door was always open, and as they passed by, there he sat in full view and with a magnificent glower masking his features. Under these circumstances, the writers felt cheap and undeserving of their money until they managed to figure out that this was exactly what Sennett wanted them to feel. After that point, the gag men had their boss right where they wanted him.

If the writers had a full story treatment finished, Sennett received only a portion at a time. The remainder was held back as long as possible. Any logical excuse which could be stretched out into several weeks was welcomed. Such was the case with the new cafeteria which Sennett wanted to build. He made the mistake of consulting his writing staff for their suggestions on what to name it. They milked that problem for all it was worth in terms of passing the time of day. Whenever he accosted one of the staff, they immediately gave him a new suggestion for a name, trying to distract him as much as possible from the business at hand. When both sides of the coin are adequately weighed, it appears to have been a draw for each. Sennett gave his writers headaches and they returned them.

Although Sennett was conscious of his cultural limitations, he was capable of forming close attachments with anyone. He possessed a deep affection for his company, and the faithful were rewarded with a firm friendship that often bordered on true affection. On the other hand, those who chose to leave Keystone were viewed as traitors, and in some cases, even cut off from social friendship by Sennett.

His sense of the public taste had become formalized by 1914. From that time on, Sennett often spoke of his comedy success as the application of a carefully thought-out theory. The essence of Sennett's comedy revolved around his professional viewpoint that tragedy was the basis of all true comedy. Take a tragic situation, add ludicrous touches of unreality, and exaggerate—that was his theory in a capsule. One final touch which he insisted upon was romance. Regardless of how foolish the plot might be, romance served as the unifying factor. Different elements appealed to different persons, but Sennett felt that romance was an experience common to everyone. If nothing else between the opening and closing titles came close to their real life, love did. At one time or another, it had touched every person in the audience. Romance became a hinge for any and all to identify with the Keystone antics.

Sennett claimed to have thought out all of these ideas in the bathtub. It seems difficult to believe of a grown man, but he actually had a bathtub in his office. When the tower was constructed in late 1912, Sennett had the tub installed. In his autobiography, he mentioned that the possession of his own office bathtub was an achievement of which he had long dreamed. For some men, the golf links or a steam bath provided the necessary stimulus for fruitful thinking and at the same time offered a measure of relaxation. For Sennett, it seems to have been a bath that put him in the mood to think, and a number of people who worked with him will swear that he actually used the tub, soaking for hours at a time while looking out over the studio and musing over various problems that had arisen. And he did have his problems.

One of them was the safety of his personnel. Life at Keystone was somewhat hazardous, but it was seldom that anyone was seriously injured. Every possible precaution was taken to prevent accidents; nonetheless, accidents did still happen. When a bad accident occurred, things became pretty quiet around the studio until the shock wore off. No trouper liked to see one of his own meet with death or with a crippling injury, and Sennett took it as hard as anyone else.

Walter Wright had taken a crew to Santa Monica to shoot some scenes of a road race for incorporation into *Skidding Hearts*. Lewis Jackson, an ace driver and chauffeur for the Universal serial team of Cunard and Ford, was entered in the competition. A rather large crowd was on hand for the race and witnessed the tragedy of Jackson as he lost control of his vehicle and shot headlong into a cluster of four trees. The racing car exploded, killing its driver instantly. Portions of the car flew in all directions, killing a female patron of a soda stand and one spectator. The main part of the car—or what was left of it—glanced off the trees and struck down L. B. Jenkins, who had filmed the event up to the moment he was hit. Jenkins also died instantly and his camera was totally demolished.

Fatal accidents such as this one were a rare occurrence at Keystone, regardless of the picture which had been painted over the years of the utter disregard for life and limb which the early movie industry had. The studio personnel collected $462 to present to Jenkins' widow, who had filed with the state of California for compensation, naming the Keystone Film Company as defendant. Sennett sent a large floral tribute in the form of a camera and tripod to rest on the cemetery grave.

The last year with Keystone had been the roughest. Beside the infighting with Aitken and his group at Triangle, there had been the usual problems at the studio and a few new ones. *Mickey* had finally been finished at a cost of $125,000 of Kessel's and Bauman's money. Sennett had dipped into his own funds and paid out personal money to keep things going when New York periodically balked at paying the bills. Sennett's personal relationship with Mabel was finished, and she had left the lot. Chaplin, Arbuckle, and now Mabel—gone. Al St. John had left to join Arbuckle, and Charles Arling and Hank Mann had joined the new Fox program, which was producing two-reel comedies for release in early 1917.

During 1915, Sennett had found that pretty girls added to both his films and his advertising material.[1] It was always a more interesting scene when his comedians were surrounded by a bevy of youthful beauties. Newspapers and magazines were more likely to use such pictures, giving Keystone free publicity. As a result of this discovery, the Sennett Bathing Beauties came into existence. They were clothed in the most daring of swimsuits possible fifty years ago,[2] and Sennett publicity pictures began to receive much more attention by the news media. The lucky girls chosen for the Bathing Beauties were paid $12 weekly to exhibit their charms for the Keystone cameras.

One girl who joined this cinematic chorus was to reach the top quickly. Gloria Swanson had worked on the Essanay lot and while

[1] An early example of this kind of cheesecake was the pajama parade in a girls' dormitory featured in *Those College Girls*.

[2] The bathing suits were usually one or two inches shorter than the prevailing style. Although daring for the time, they were always in excellent taste. Vulgarity in this instance was not tolerated.

Gloria Swanson's radiant beauty is well exemplified in this scene from *Danger Girl*.

*Ambrose's Cup of Woe* is full. Mack Swain registers shock at the sight in the artist's studio. Minta Durfee is the model.

there, met another comic, Wallace Beery. They were married in March, 1916, and separated a month later when both joined Keystone. Gloria posed for bathing-beauty publicity pictures but bypassed the chorus line and was first starred in *A Dash of Courage*, a May release. She had signed for leading roles at $65 weekly, with her husband receiving $50 per week.[3] Miss Swanson was very ambitious and possessed genuine acting talent as well as beauty. She was quickly paired off with Bobby Vernon, a juvenile actor on the lot, and Teddy the Keystone dog.[4] Between them, a new type of comic melodrama emerged. Bobby played the errant and fleeting boy friend who woke up to true love when he found his sweet girl friend in deadly danger (amidst much comic action).

Many girls broke into the Bathing Beauty line-up only to be promoted to featured roles, much as some of the early Kops had been. Mary Thurman had been born in Richfield, Utah, in 1894. After graduation from the University of Utah, she migrated to California as a schoolteacher. For summer employment, she went to the Triangle studio and was given a role in *Sunshine Dad*. Sennett signed her and by 1920, she was playing in William S. Hart westerns.

Marie Prevost was another early Sennett Bathing Beauty who would become a great success in features. Born in Sarnia, Canada, she was educated in Denver and entered movies in a manner in which most schoolgirls dreamed of. In 1917, she paid a visit to a friend who was working on the Keystone lot and was immediately asked to sign a contract. After being featured for a few years in Sennett comedies, Marie followed the footsteps of Bebe Daniels (who had left Harold Lloyd for features) and Gloria Swanson, moving off for greener pastures in light and frothy feature comedies, such as Ernst Lubitsch's *The Marriage Circle*. Her ending was quite tragic; she died suddenly at the height of her career.

[3] Keystone kept track of idle time, that is, time during which the actors were not working for any reason. Idle time was an economic loss, and interestingly enough, Beery's stay on the lot placed him at the head of this list.

[4] Teddy was the second dog to win fame at Keystone. The first had been Fido, featured with Arbuckle in many comedies. Teddy became so popular with audiences that when he died, the public was not informed. Without any fanfare, Sennett used the services of three other Great Danes to carry on for Teddy.

The grotesque comedian was going out of vogue. Outrageous make-up was being played down, and the participants in Sennett films were playing their roles with an appearance of being normal, every-day human beings. Of course, those comics who had already been accepted by the public (such as Mack Swain and Chester Conklin) remained in their famous garb, but even these comedians altered their appearance somewhat. The moustaches became smaller and neater; the clothing had a much better fit to it. During its last year of existence, Keystone madness was in the process of being toned down to become even more methodical but also more reasonable. The change in public taste anticipated by this alteration in style would show up clearly in the Paramount-Sennett comedies of 1918–19.

New comics joined the organization during 1916–17; some became famous, others played their roles and faded back into obscurity. In the fall of 1916, Walter Wright was directing a picture with a circus background. The Sells-Floto Circus was about to settle into winter quarters and allowed Wright to film his scenes on their grounds. When he returned to the Keystone lot, the director advised Sennett that he had discovered two personalities worth signing to a contract. Sennett took his advice and in December signed Grace De Garro and Harry Bayfield to enter his employ at the Fun Factory. De Garro was an acrobat with the De Garro Troupe, and Bayfield was the head clown of Sells-Floto.

One unusual little fellow signed with Keystone in 1917. He would become the greatest money-maker on the lot within two years, and a star in Sennett comedies over the next decade. His background was not out of the ordinary, nor would it have given any indication of the fame and fortune ahead. In 1907, he had stepped from Sam T. Jack's burlesque in Chicago to the Essanay Company, where he had spent two years sweeping floors and playing occasional roles in comedies. Not exactly a sensation, he left in 1909 to return to the boards. A second venture with Essanay brought little additional distinction, and it is more than likely that he might never have achieved much more in the Essanay ranks had it not been for Charles Chaplin.

Ben Turpin was selected by Chaplin to appear in the first two comedies he made under his new Essanay contract. When Samuel S. Hutchinson formed Vogue in October, 1915, to replace the Keystone brand at Mutual, Turpin was among the first comics to be hired. Ben signed on at $100 weekly and with Rube Miller and Paddy McGuire, kept the Vogue brand afloat for a few months. Turpin's Vogue films were hardly what one could describe as outstanding. They were merely knockabout slapstick films that had no particular charm about them. Ben's greatest asset, his crossed eyes, were used sparingly and his pacing seems to have been erratic. Whether this was his fault or that of his director is a moot question, but there was little to set him apart from any other slapstick comic at the time.

It was his first contract with Keystone that made the difference. Here, Turpin was with the real professionals—men who knew how to make others laugh and who had made the study of humor a science. He made a couple of appearances before being handed the lead in *A Clever Dummy*. Turpin was the entire show in this excellent burlesque and now seemed to be headed in the right direction. His ability to do a backward somersault (known as a "108" in the trade) and his crossed eyes were accentuated in the Keystones. Pacing was equally important, and the rapid-fire but often spasmodic tempo of the Vogue comedies was replaced by that certain Keystone touch. Ben Turpin had found a home where he was appreciated and valued. The little Frenchman plunged into his work with zest, and the low-burlesque charades which he created were to become gems of visual comedy, remembered and revered through the years.

The last days of Keystone were Turpin's initiation into that peculiar but profitable brand of humor that belonged to Sennett's studio. His greatest fame was yet to come with the Pathé releases of the twenties, but it was during the finale of the greatest comedy organization in screen history that Ben Turpin relearned his trade—how to earn money by making people laugh.

Of all the comic stars whom Sennett discovered or trained during the active years at Keystone, only a small handful went on to achieve greater fame than they had experienced while at Keystone. Charles Chaplin is the outstanding example. Had Chaplin conformed to the organized lunacy of Keystone, there is serious reason to doubt that the immense success he achieved would ever have come his way. Keystone was too restrictive for a comedian of his ability and temperament. It had to be restrictive to achieve any degree of the production which a comedy-hungry market demanded. Neither Keystone time nor Keystone money was available to treat the business of making films as Chaplin wished.

Mabel Normand ranked closest to Chaplin in talent, yet she achieved a good deal less than prognosticators of 1915 would have believed. The downward spiral of her career seemed to be the result of her personal affairs, which had an important bearing on her health and her work, not a result of a lack of talent. Although she made at least three feature comedies which are today considered minor classics, Mabel's career was finished for all practical purposes the day that she passed through the Keystone portals to work for Goldwyn.

Chester Conklin, Mack Swain, Hank Mann, and Al St. John all left Sennett for good to headline their own series throughout the twenties for Fox, Standard Cinema, and various independents. Yet none were really able to enjoy the widespread adulation to which they had been subjected while at Keystone. On the distaff side, youthful Juanita Hansen left for much greater fame as a Pathé serial queen, but her career had been destroyed by 1922.[5] Her tragic story was not repeated by Gloria Swanson. Miss Swanson was a woman driven by an intense ambition to succeed as a serious actress—an ambition which she fulfilled completely under the guidance of Cecil B. de Mille.

Based on discussions with several of the Keystone comedians still living, I have come to the conclusion that more than talent, ambition was the prime key to success. This is hardly a startling observation, since many personalities of limited talent were top box-office figures in the motion-picture business, but it needs to

[5] See *Continued Next Week: A History of the Moving Picture Serial* (University of Oklahoma Press, 1964).

be re-emphasized. Today, we all too often equate success with talent—an equation that has very little validity.

There was really nothing more magical about Keystone than the wacky turns which its comedy took. As a unit, the individuals functioned well. On their own, they either tried out their own ideas of comedy, or they were simply satisfied with earning their $500–$800 weekly with no interest in trying to fill the shoes of a Chaplin, Keaton, or Lloyd. Few of these comedians had ever earned that kind of money before, and they realized that it was better pay than they could hope to receive in any other occupation. From humble backgrounds, these comedians with a limited amount of success had enough to cope with as it was. They could always point to Chaplin, whose personal life was in a state of near-constant confusion. A public figure of immense proportions, his every move was watched with eagle eyes.

These lesser comedians possessed their share of problems with which to live. As with many others in the world of make-believe, the bottle proved to be the downfall of some. Among others, Al St. John was ruined by a fixation for alcohol. A clever comic with a youthful appearance, St. John's native athletic ability made him a natural knockabout comedian. He joined Keystone as a wide-eyed Kop in 1913 after a career that had included a background in musical comedy. He was one of the fortunate few whose marriage lasted through thick and thin, good times and bad, until his death in 1962. Flora St. John was devoted to her husband and is presently in the process of establishing a museum in his memory at her home in Florida. Al's bouts with the bottle finally reduced him to second- and third-rate roles. Throughout the sound era, he was cast as "Fuzzy" St. John, the comic side-kick of many singing cowboys.

In those days of free and easy living, it might well be expected that sex would have reared its head at the Keystone studio. Other studios were notorious for such, but Sennett worked hard to run a clean show all the way. Although an exception had been made in the case of Joe Jackson and his liquor supply, Sennett made no exceptions in the realm of male-female relationships. Either everything was above board or the party in question left immediately. What the comics did once the working day was over and they had left the lot, Sennett rightly felt was none of his business. As long as the comedians kept their personal life in sufficient order to work every day, Sennett displayed no displeasure at the stories which filtered back to his ears; he was no saint himself.

Sennett was proud of his studio and of its success. He went out of his way to make certain that no incident upset its smooth operation. One humorous occasion did present itself when an industry censorship group sent a team of inspectors around to the various lots. Sennett proudly escorted them on a tour of the studio, and as he threw open each dressing-room door, he exclaimed happily, "See? No sex on Sennett's lot." Imagine his surprise as he threw open the final door, made his stock comment, and looked inside to see a naked actress on the lap of an equally naked comedian. The man was dismissed that same day.

Although the Keystone Film Company officially died in 1917, the films produced by Keystone did not meet with the same fate. As previously mentioned, Keystone comedies produced for Mutual release were duped and re-duped by Mutual in a clandestine attempt to retain the use of footage for which a demand still existed. With the sale of the New York Motion Picture Company to Triangle, the reproduction rights of the Mutual Keystones fell into Harry Aitken's control. But many of the early Keystones had not been protected by copyright and thus became fair game for duping by anyone wishing to do so. As the prints circulating within the continental United States wore to the point where duping was no longer feasible, a profitable trade arose in Europe. Release prints which had been sold on the export market were duped with English titles (or with none at all) and brought back into the United States to supply a demand which existed long after the Keystone Film Company ceased to function.

Toward the closing days of the Triangle organization, Harry Aitken re-released some of the Keystone comedies. When Triangle collapsed in 1918, Smithers and Company stepped in and took charge. J. R. Naulty, former head of the Triangle Exchange system,

Lovely Juanita Hansen and her dashing beau Bobby Vernon have aroused the suspicions of Ford Sterling and his Keystone Kops in *His Pride and Shame* (1916).

Mary Thurman and Al St. John ham it up in a Keystone-Triangle farce of prehistoric life in *The Stone Age*.

replaced Aitken as president. The bankers placed Triangle's vault up for auction, and most of the negatives were bought by independent distributing firms. Aitken managed to buy the rights to certain negatives and tried another revival under the auspices of Tri-Stone Pictures in 1923. Although a limited market still existed, Tri-Stone was a failure for many reasons. More success was to meet the efforts of certain state-right distributors such as W. H. Productions, Jans Producing Corporation, and the Tower Film Corporation. Armed with a large number of re-edited Keystone comedies, they arose in 1918 to fill a distinct need for comedies on the market.

Many of the producing companies had been shut down by the influenza epidemic of 1918. Theaters across the nation also closed, but when the epidemic was over, a number of the smaller producers were unable to resume production. Financed to the extreme, they were hard pressed to survive the halt in production flow, and their inability to pay the obligations on their debts brought an end to their activities. This created a rather large gap, for comedies had been in relatively short supply prior to the flu epidemic.

The newly formed distributing firms had bought the rights to many of the Keystone comedies. They struck new negatives and placed the comedies on the independent market. In deference to the war fervor, W. H. Productions named their releases "Eagle" or "Liberty" Keystones. The new prints were sold to exchanges at $80 per single reel. They were then rented to exhibitors and bookings were fast and furious; the Keystones still held a fascination for patrons.

An interesting example is provided by the Gardiner Syndicate of Buffalo, New York. T. R. Gardiner purchased 750 reels from W. H. Productions in June, 1918, at a cost of $60,000. Gardiner's purchase gave him the exclusive right to distribute the re-edited Keystones in New York state. One year later, his prints were worn to the point where circulation was no longer feasible. He then paid W. H. Productions another $60,000 for a complete set of 750 new prints.

A hue and cry went up from other competition until distributors finally asked the Federal Trade Commission for an injunction against W. H. Productions. Their complaint alleged that the public was being duped into believing that there were new comedies and asked that if re-editing of these films was to continue, W. H. Productions be required to display the old title as well as the new one.

In this particular case, the Federal Trade Commission was not as impotent as some of its historical critics have claimed, and it did act. But W. H. Productions caused the proceedings to be terminated by entry of a consent order on an agreed statement of facts. This meant in effect that the distributor agreed to point out to the public that the films were re-releases. Each one then carried both the old and the new title.

W. H. Productions is another deep and fascinating mystery. Although neither Harry Aitken nor Adam Kessel were ever mentioned publicly as participating in the firm, there was some reason to believe that Aitken at least was involved behind the scenes. Ostensibly, Joseph Simmonds was listed as president. Elmer J. McGovern, a former assistant to Kessel, held the position of production editor, and H. J. Shepard served as advertising manager and spokesman for the corporation. Hal Reid did the re-editing of all W. H. Productions' releases.

Whereas Jans Producing Corporation released old films made by a variety of firms, the entire inventory handled by W. H. Productions came from the companies previously owned and operated by Kessel and Bauman and Harry Aitken. When the corporation began operations in late 1917, its prospectus listed financial backing which had once heavily supported Aitken. Foreign rights were handled by Western Import of London under the direction of Roy Aitken.

Suspicions were confirmed in 1921 when the management of Triangle was finally able to unravel the long history of complicated financial maneuvering by the former president. Harry Aitken. Named defendants in a million-dollar suit, the Aitken brothers were charged, among other things, with selling Triangle assets valued at $500,000 to the Tower Film Corporation and W. H. Productions for $100,000. This in itself would have been considered no more than poor business judgment, except for one fact

—Harry and Roy Aitken had organized and owned both companies. Thus, while liquidation of Triangle assets in 1917–18 had ostensibly been done to relieve an awkward financial position, in fact it served to enrich the Aitken brothers and staved off the inevitable reckoning for a few years.

And so, the Keystone comedies gradually passed from the scene, long after their actual production ceased. They had accomplished a great deal in five short years. A new form of screen comedy had burst forth on the American motion-picture screen, lighting the way for others as it created a legend in the hearts of theater patrons the world over. But humor on the screen had evolved, moving forth under the guiding hand of the one man, Mack Sennett, who had done so much for it. In reality, the Keystones were an anachronism by 1920.

Due to higher rental fees and better distribution through Pathé, Sennett was to make more money in the twenties with fewer comedies,[6] but he never again achieved the popularity of those Keystone years. His films lost much of the ingenuity which had marked his early years. They became stamped with the assembly-line look which distinguished all of the silent comedy shorts in the twenties. But the Keystones have immeasurable worth for the historian as documents of social values. They stand alone as the best examples of social satire of an age and a time long gone. Many have vanished unto dust, but those which remain recall fond memories of the Fun Factory.

[6] It has been estimated that Mack Sennett lost somewhere between $5,000,000 and $8,000,000 in the stock market crash of 1929.

# Epilogue

I<small>T HAS BEEN FIFTY YEARS</small> since the Keystone Film Company was dissolved. In those fifty years much has happened, yet the name Keystone still evokes a fond response. Slapstick comedy is now referred to as being in the Keystone tradition. The custard pie and the unforgettable antics of the Kops are with us today in memory. Occasionally, a Hollywood showman will produce a film on the order of *It's a Mad, Mad, Mad, Mad World* or *Those Magnificent Men in Their Flying Machines*, and over the roar of audience laughter, critics can be heard crying, "Shades of Keystone and Mack Sennett!"

Fortunately for future generations, a representative number of the Keystone comedies are still in existence. Through the efforts of individual film collectors, firms dedicated to reproducing the old silent films for home consumption, and the Library of Congress, which has paper prints on deposit, we can still view the comic routines which kept our parents and grandparents laughing until they cried. We can share some of the feelings and experiences that they had many years before we were born.

The Keystones symbolize a transition of screen comedy from the rather crude state of a new industry's early growth to the polished, sophisticated product of a mature entertainment form.

169

Screen comedy advanced immeasurably because of the Keystone contribution, and the comedies remain today as a reflection of an era. Through the Keystone comedies, we are able to gain an insight into a generation long past—its follies, foibles, and fashions. Underneath the savage satire and frenzied farce, there are overtones of a people whose problems were as close and great to them as ours are to us.

But they were more fortunate than their offspring, for the Keystone comedies helped to provide a release from worldly cares that we will never know. We are unabashedly pseudosophisticated, but we have lost something along the way. Our generation has lost the ability to laugh at itself—an ability which helped our forefathers to keep themselves and the world around them in proper perspective.

The film-collecting hobby is a rapidly growing one, and many of today's young people express a loving fondness for the small strips of celluloid from which small but distinguishable figures dance across the screen in comic routines conceived many, many years ago. Because of these young people, the figures will continue to flit to and fro on a thin beam of light, their key to immortality.

These never-to-be-forgotten shadows will dance forever, to delight audiences again and again. Regardless of the intellectual scorn directed at slapstick in our world of today, it lives on in a few routines created by Red Skelton and Soupy Sales, and it lives on in the long-ago world of Keystone and Mack Sennett, a world where Kops and custards reigned supreme.

# Appendix: The Keystone Comedies

On the following pages, the reader will find a complete listing of the Keystone comedies and of the actors and actresses who appeared in them. Credits for the years 1912, 1913, and a portion of 1914 are vague because few reviews mentioned them and most of the scripts are gone. Credits were not given on the films themselves, and since many of them are no longer available for viewing, that avenue has been closed by time. It can be assumed, however, that Sennett directed all of the releases through January, 1913. From that point on, Henry Lehrman shared directorial duties with Sennett until Wilfred Lucas and George Nichols joined in mid-1913. Robert Thornby did the "Little Billy" Jacobs comedies, and Charles Avery is known to have directed thirty-one of the early Arbuckle Keystones, along with the "Hogan" series and seven of Syd Chaplin's films. Toward the end of 1914, Ford Sterling, Mabel Normand, Roscoe Arbuckle, and Charles Chaplin directed many of their own comedies.

The Triangle-Keystone comedies were much better documented during their first year, but after that they were also neglected by contemporary source materials. Where possible, the available credits have been given from scripts. Until publication of this index, the only attempt at a compilation of this sort was to be found in Davide Turconi's *Mack Sennett,* a volume published in Italy during 1961. This present index surpasses Turconi's in completeness of titles and credits. Much credit belongs to Samuel Gill for his assistance in locating certain production data.

## KEYSTONE COMEDIES
### *1912*

**SEPTEMBER**

23 *Cohen Collects a Debt* ½r
Fred Mace, Ford Sterling
*The Water Nymph* ½r
Mabel Normand, Ford Sterling, Fred Mace

30 *Riley and Schultz* ½r
Ford Sterling, Fred Mace
*The New Neighbor* ½r
Fred Mace, Ford Sterling, Mabel Normand

**OCTOBER**

7 *The Beating He Needed* ½r
Fred Mace, Ford Sterling
*Pedro's Dilemma* ½r
Mack Sennett, Mabel Normand, Ford Sterling, Fred Mace, Victoria Forde

14 *Stolen Glory* 1r
Mack Sennett, Mabel Normand, Ford Sterling, Fred Mace

21 *Ambitious Butler* ½r
Mack Sennett, Mabel Normand, Ford Sterling, Fred Mace
*The Flirting Husband* ½r
Mabel Normand, Ford Sterling

28 *The Grocery Clerk's Romance* ½r
Ford Sterling
*[Cohen] At Coney Island* ½r
Mack Sennett, Mabel Normand, Ford Sterling

**NOVEMBER**

4 *Mabel's Lovers* ½r
Mabel Normand, Fred Mace, Alice Davenport
*At It Again* ½r
Fred Mace, Mack Sennett, Ford Sterling, Mabel Normand

11 *The Deacon's Trouble* ½r
Mabel Normand, Ford Sterling, Fred Mace
*A Temperamental Husband* ½r
Mabel Normand, Ford Sterling, Fred Mace

18 *The Rivals* ½r
Mack Sennett, Mabel Normand, Ford Sterling
*Mr. Fix-It* ½r
Mack Sennett, Mabel Normand, Ford Sterling, Fred Mace

25 *A Desperate Lover* ½r
Fred Mace, Mabel Normand
*A Bear Escape* ½r
Mack Sennett, Fred Mace,
Ford Sterling

DECEMBER

2 *Pat's Day Off* ½r
Mack Sennett, Fred Mace,
Ford Sterling
*Brown's Séance* ½r
Mabel Normand

9 *A Family Mix-up* ½r
Mack Sennett, Fred Mace,
Mabel Normand
*A Midnight Elopement* ½r

Ford Sterling, Mabel Nor-
mand

16 *Mabel's Adventures* ½r
Mabel Normand, Fred Mace,
Ford Sterling
*Useful Sheep* ½r
[An educational short sub-
ject]

23 *Hoffmeyer's Legacy* ½r
Ford Sterling, Fred Mace
*Drummer's Vacation* ½r
Fred Mace, Alice Davenport

30 *The Duel* ½r
Mack Sennett, Mabel Nor-
mand
*Mabel's Stratagem* ½r
Mabel Normand, Fred Mace

## *1913*

JANUARY

6 *Saving Mabel's Dad* ½r
Fred Mace, Mabel Normand
*A Double Wedding* ½r
Ford Sterling, Fred Mace

13 *The Cure That Failed* ½r
Mabel Normand, Ford Ster-
ling, Fred Mace
*How Hiram Won Out* ½r
Ford Sterling

20 *Sir Thomas Lipton Out West*
½r [An educational short
subject]
*For Lizzie's Sake* ½r

27 *The Mistaken Masher* ½r
Ford Sterling, Mabel Nor-
mand, Mack Sennett
*The Deacon Outwitted* ½r

Mabel Normand, Ford Ster-
ling

FEBRUARY

3 *The Elite Ball* ½r
Ford Sterling, Fred Mace
*Just Brown's Luck* ½r
Ford Sterling, Fred Mace,
Mabel Normand, Alice Dav-
enport

6 *The Battle of Who Run* 1r
Mack Sennett, Fred Mace,
Ford Sterling, Mabel Nor-
mand

10 *The Jealous Waiter* ½r
*The Stolen Purse* ½r
Mack Sennett, Fred Mace,
Ford Sterling

13 *Heinze's Resurrection* 1r

Ford Sterling, Mabel Normand, Fred Mace

17 *Mabel's Heroes* ½r
Mabel Normand, Mack Sennett, Fred Mace, Nick Cogley
*Her Birthday Present* ½r
Fred Mace

20 *A Landlord's Troubles* ½r
Ford Sterling
*Forced Bravery* ½r

24 *The Professor's Daughter* ½r
Mabel Normand, Ford Sterling, Fred Mace
*A Tangled Affair* ½r
Mabel Normand

27 *A Red Hot Romance* ½r
Mabel Normand, Fred Mace, Ford Sterling
*A Doctored Affair* ½r
Mabel Normand

**MARCH**

3 *The Sleuth's Last Stand* ½r
Mack Sennett, Fred Mace
*A Deaf Burglar* ½r
Fred Mace, Charles Avery

6 *The Sleuths at the Floral Parade* ½r
Mack Sennett, Fred Mace, Ford Sterling, Mabel Normand
*The Rural Third Degree* ½r
Mabel Normand, Fred Mace

10 *A Strong Revenge* 1r
Mack Sennett, Mabel Normand, Ford Sterling

13 *The Two Widows* ½r
Ford Sterling

*Foiling Fickle Father* ½r
Mabel Normand

17 *Love and Pain* ½r
*The Man Next Door* ½r
Ford Sterling, Fred Mace

20 *A Wife Wanted* ½r
Dot Farley
*The Rube and the Baron* ½r
Mack Sennett, Fred Mace, Ford Sterling, Mabel Normand

24 *Jenny's Pearls* ½r
Fred Mace
*The Chief's Predicament* ½r

27 *At Twelve O'Clock* 1r
Mabel Normand, Fred Mace, Mack Sennett

31 *Her New Beau* ½r
Directed by Lehrman
Mabel Normand, Fred Mace, Mack Sennett
*On His Wedding Day* ½r
Ford Sterling

**APRIL**

3 *The Land Salesman* ½r
Ford Sterling
*Hide and Seek* ½r

7 *Those Good Old Days* 1r
Mabel Normand

10 *A Game of Poker* ½r
Ford Sterling
*Father's Choice* ½r
Mabel Normand, Ford Sterling

14 *A Life in the Balance* 1r
Directed by Sennett

Ford Sterling, Dot Farley
17 *Murphy's IOU*  ½r
Directed by Lehrman
Ford Sterling
*A Dollar Did It*  ½r
Directed by Lehrman
21 *Cupid in a Dental Parlor*  1r
Directed by Lehrman
Fred Mace
24 *A Fishy Affair*  ½r
Directed by Sennett
Ford Sterling
*The Bangville Police*  ½r
Directed by Lehrman
Fred Mace
28 *The New Conductor*  ½r
Directed by Sennett
Ford Sterling
*His Chum the Baron*  ½r
Directed by Sennett

**MAY**

 1 *The Ragtime Band*  1r
Directed by Sennett
Mabel Normand, Ford Sterling
[Reissued as *The Jazz Band* by W. H. Productions]
 5 *Algy on the Force*  ½r
Directed by Lehrman
Fred Mace
*His Ups and Downs*  ½r
Directed by Sennett
Ford Sterling
 8 *The Darktown Belle*  ½r
Directed by Lehrman
Fred Mace
*A Little Hero*  ½r
Directed by Sennett

Mabel Normand
12 *Mabel's Awful Mistake*  1r
Directed by Sennett
Mack Sennett, Mabel Normand
[Reissued as *Her Deceitful Lover* by W. H. Productions]
15 *Their First Execution*  1r
Directed by Sennett
Mack Sennett
19 *Hubby's Job*  ½r  Directed by Sennett
Fred Mace, Mabel Normand
*Twixt Love and Fire*  ½r
Directed by Lehrman
22 *The Foreman of the Jury*  1r
Directed by Sennett
Fred Mace, Mabel Normand
26 *Toplitsky and Company*  1r
Directed by Lehrman
Ford Sterling
29 *The Gangsters*  1r
Directed by Lehrman
Fred Mace, Roscoe Arbuckle

**JUNE**

 3 *Barney Oldfield's Race for a Life*  1r  Directed by Sennett
Mack Sennett, Mabel Normand, Ford Sterling, Barney Oldfield
 5 *Passions, He Had Three*  ½r
Directed by Lehrman
Roscoe Arbuckle
*Help! Help! Hydrophobia!*  ½r  Directed by Lehrman
Roscoe Arbuckle
 9 *The Hansom Driver*  ½r

Directed by Sennett
Mack Sennett, Ford Sterling,
Mabel Normand
*Feeding Time* ½r
Directed by Lehrman
[An educational short subject]

12 *The Speed Queen* 1r
Directed by Sennett
Mabel Normand, Ford Sterling, Nick Cogley

16 *The Waiters' Picnic* 1r
Directed by Sennett
Mabel Normand, Ford Sterling, Roscoe Arbuckle

19 *Out and In* ½r Directed
by Lehrman
Ford Sterling
*The Tale of a Black Eye* ½r
Fred Mace

23 *A Bandit* ½r Directed by
Sennett
Roscoe Arbuckle
*Peeping Pete* ½r Directed
Mack Sennett, Ford Sterling

26 *His Crooked Career* ⅔r
Directed by Sennett
Mack Sennett, Ford Sterling
*The Largest Boat Ever
Launched Sideways* ⅓r
Directed by Sennett
[An educational short subject]

30 *For the Love of Mabel* 1r
Directed by Lehrman
Mabel Normand, Roscoe Arbuckle

JULY

3 *Rastus and the Game Cock*
1r Directed by Sennett

7 *Safe in Jail* 1r Directed by
Sennett
Ford Sterling

10 *The Telltale Light* 1r
Directed by Sennett
Mabel Normand, Roscoe Arbuckle, Charles Avery, Alice Davenport

14 *Love and Rubbish* 1r
Directed by Lehrman
Ford Sterling

17 *A Noise from the Deep* 1r
Directed by Sennett
Roscoe Arbuckle, Mabel Normand

21 *The Peddler* ½r Directed
by Lehrman
Ford Sterling
*Love and Courage* ½r
Directed by Lehrman
Roscoe Arbuckle, Mabel Normand

24 *Get Rich Quick* 1r
Directed by Lucas

28 *Just Kids* 1r Directed by
Lehrman

31 *Professor Bean's Removal*
1r Directed by Lehrman
Mabel Normand, Ford Sterling

AUGUST

4 *Cohen's Outing* 1r
Directed by Lucas
Ford Sterling, Charles Avery,

Alice Davenport, Wilfred Lucas

7 *A Game of Pool*  ½r
Directed by Lucas
Ford Sterling
*The Latest in Life Saving*
½r  Directed by Lucas
[An educational short subject]

11 *The Riot*  1r  Directed by Sennett
Roscoe Arbuckle, Ford Sterling, Mabel Normand

14 *A Chip Off the Old Block*
1r  Directed by Lehrman

21 *The Firebugs*  2r  Directed by Sennett
Ford Sterling, Fred Mace

25 *Baby Day*  1r  Directed by Lucas
Mabel Normand, Ford Sterling
*The Kelp Industry*  1r
[An educational short subject]

28 *Mabel's New Hero*  1r
Directed by Sennett
Roscoe Arbuckle, Mabel Normand

SEPTEMBER

1 *Fatty's Day Off*  ½r
Directed by Lucas
Roscoe Arbuckle
*Los Angeles Harbor, California*  ½r  Directed by Lucas
[An educational short subject]

4 *The New Baby*  1r
Directed by Lehrman

8 *Mabel's Dramatic Career*
1r  Directed by Sennett
Mack Sennett, Mabel Normand, Ford Sterling, Roscoe Arbuckle
[Reissued as *Her Dramatic Debut* by W.H. Productions]

11 *The Gypsy Queen*  1r
Directed by Sennett
Mabel Normand, Roscoe Arbuckle

15 *What Father Saw*  ½r
Directed by Lucas
*Willie Minds the Dog*  ½r
Directed by Lucas

18 *The Faithful Taxicab*  1r
Directed by Sennett
Ford Sterling, Mabel Normand, Roscoe Arbuckle

22 *When Dreams Come True*
1r  Directed by Sennett
Ford Sterling

25 *Mother's Boy*  1r  Directed by Lehrman
Roscoe Arbuckle, Nick Cogley

27 *The Bowling Match*  1r
Directed by Sennett
Mabel Normand, Ford Sterling

OCTOBER

2 *Billy Dodges Bills*  1r
Directed by Lucas

6 *Across the Alley*  ½r
Directed by Lucas
*The Abalone Industry*  ½r

177

Directed by Lehrman
[An educational short subject]

9 *Schnitz the Tailor* 1r
Directed by Sennett
Ford Sterling

13 *Their Husbands* 1r
Directed by Lucas

16 *A Healthy Neighborhood* 1r
Directed by Sennett
Ford Sterling

20 *Two Old Tars* 1r Directed by Lehrman

23 *A Quiet Little Wedding* 1r
Directed by Lucas
Roscoe Arbuckle

27 *The Janitor* ½r Directed by Lucas
*Making an Auto Tire* ½r
Directed by Lucas
[An educational short subject]

30 *Teddy Telzlaff and Earl Cooper, Speed Kings* 1r
Mabel Normand, Ford Sterling, Earl Cooper, Teddy Telzlaff

NOVEMBER

3 *Fatty at San Diego* 1r
Directed by Nichols
Roscoe Arbuckle

6 *Love Sickness at Sea* 1r
Directed by Sennett
Mack Sennett, Mabel Normand, Ford Sterling

10 *A Small Time Act* ½r
Directed by Nichols
Ford Sterling

*The Milk We Drink* ½r
Directed by Lucas
[An educational short subject]

13 *Wine* 1r Directed by Nichols
[An educational short subject]

17 *Our Children* 1r
[Keystone's first kiddie comedy]

20 *A Muddy Romance* 1r
Directed by Sennett
Mabel Normand, Ford Sterling
[Reissued as *Muddled in Mud* by W. H. Productions]

24 *Fatty Joins the Force* 1r
Directed by Nichols
Roscoe Arbuckle

27 *Cohen Saves the Flag* 1r
Directed by Sennett
Ford Sterling, Mabel Normand

DECEMBER

1 *The Woman Haters* 1r
Directed by Lehrman
Roscoe Arbuckle

4 *The Rogues' Gallery* ½r
Directed by Lucas
[An educational short subject]
*San Francisco Celebration* ½r Directed by Lehrman
[An educational short subject]

8 *A Ride for a Bride* 1r
Directed by Nichols

11 *The Horse Thief* 1r
Directed by Lucas
[Keystone kiddie comedy]
15 *The Gusher* 1r Directed
by Sennett
Ford Sterling, Mabel Nor-
mand
18 *Fatty's Flirtation* ½r
Directed by Nichols
Roscoe Arbuckle, Mabel Nor-
mand
*Protecting San Francisco from
Fire* ½r Directed by
Lehrman
[An educational short sub-
ject]
20 *His Sister's Kids* 1r

Directed by Nichols
22 *A Bad Game* 1r Directed
by Sennett
Ford Sterling
24 *Zuzu, the Band Leader* 2r
Directed by Sennett
Ford Sterling, Mabel Nor-
mand, Charles Haggerty
25 *Some Nerve* 1r Directed
by Sennett
Ford Sterling
27 *The Champion* 1r
Directed by Lehrman
Mabel Normand
29 *He Would A Hunting Go* 1r
Directed by Nichols
Roscoe Arbuckle

## 1914

JANUARY

1 *A Misplaced Foot* ½r
Directed by Lucas
Mabel Normand, Roscoe Ar-
buckle, Minta Durfee
*A Glimpse of Los Angeles*
½r Directed by Lucas
Mabel Normand
[An educational short sub-
ject]
3 *Love and Dynamite* 1r
Directed by Sennett
Ford Sterling
5 *Mabel's Stormy Love Affair*
1r Directed by Nichols
Mabel Normand
*How Motion Pictures Are
Made* ½r
[An educational short sub-
ject]

8 *The Under Sheriff* 1r
Directed by Nichols
Roscoe Arbuckle
12 *A Flirt's Mistake* 1r
Directed by Nichols
Roscoe Arbuckle
15 *Moscow and Its Environs*
1r
[An educational short sub-
ject]
17 *In the Clutches of a Gang* 2r
Directed by Nichols
Ford Sterling, Hank Mann,
Roscoe Arbuckle, Rube Mil-
ler, Al St. John
19 *Too Many Brides* 1r
Directed by Sennett
Ford Sterling
[Reissued as *The Love Chase*
by W. H. Productions]

179

22 *Won in a Closet* 1r
Directed by Normand
Mabel Normand
24 *Rebecca's Wedding Day* 1r
Directed by Nichols
Roscoe Arbuckle
26 *Double Crossed* 1r
Directed by Sterling
Ford Sterling
29 *Little Billy's Triumph* 1r
Directed by Thornby
Paul Jacobs
31 *Mabel's Bare Escape* 1r
Directed by Normand
Mabel Normand

FEBRUARY

2 *Making a Living* 1r
Directed by Lehrman
Charles Chaplin, Virginia
Kirtley, Minta Durfee, Alice
Davenport, Chester Conklin,
Henry Lehrman
[Reissued as *A Busted Johnny*
by W. H. Productions]
5 *Little Billy's Strategy* 1r
Directed by Thornby
Paul Jacobs
7 *Kid Auto Races at Venice*
½r Directed by Lehrman
Charles Chaplin, Henry Lehr-
man
*Olives and Their Oil* ½r
[An educational short sub-
ject]
[Purchased from outside
source]
9 *Mabel's Strange Predicament*
1r Directed by Normand

Charles Chaplin, Mabel Nor-
mand, Alice Davenport, Har-
ry McCoy, Hank Mann, Al St.
John, Chester Conklin
12 *A Robust Romeo* 1r
Directed by Nichols
16 *Baffles, Gentleman Burglar*
2r Directed by Lehrman
Ford Sterling
19 *A Thief Catcher* 1r
Directed by Sterling
21 *Love and Gasoline* 1r
Directed by Normand
Mabel Normand
[Reissued as *The Skidding
Joy Riders* by W. H. Produc-
tions]
23 *'Twixt Love and Fire* 1r
Directed by Nichols
26 *Little Billy's City Cousin* 1r
Directed by Thornby
Paul Jacobs
28 *Between Showers* 1r
Directed by Lehrman
Charles Chaplin, Emma Clif-
ton, Ford Sterling, Chester
Conklin

MARCH

2 *A Film Johnnie* 1r
Directed by Nichols
Charles Chaplin, Virginia
Kirtley, Minta Durfee, Roscoe
Arbuckle
5 *A False Beauty* 1r
Directed by Sterling
Ford Sterling, Mack Sennett
[Reissued as *A Faded Vam-
pire* by W. H. Productions]

9 *Tango Tangles* ¾ r
Directed by Sennett
Charles Chaplin, Ford Sterling, Roscoe Arbuckle, Chester Conklin
*Washing Our Clothes* ¼ r
Directed by Sennett
[An educational short subject]

16 *His Favorite Pastime* 1r
Directed by Nichols
Charles Chaplin, Roscoe Arbuckle, Peggy Pearce

19 *A Rural Demon* 1r
Directed by Lehrman and Sennett
Roscoe Arbuckle

20 *The Race* 1r Directed by Thornby and Diamond

23 *Across the Hall* 1r
Directed by Sterling and Sennett

26 *Cruel, Cruel Love* 1r
Directed by Nichols
Charles Chaplin
[Reissued as *Lord Helpus* by W. H. Productions]

28 *Barnyard Flirtations* 1r
Directed by Arbuckle
Roscoe Arbuckle

30 *A Back Yard Theater* 1r
Directed by Diamond
Paul Jacobs and the Keystone Kids

APRIL

2 *Chicken Chaser* 1r
Directed by Arbuckle
Roscoe Arbuckle

4 *The Star Boarder* 1r
Directed by Nichols
Charles Chaplin, Edgar Kennedy, Alice Davenport, Gordon Griffith

6 *Mack at It Again* 1r
Directed by Sennett
Mack Sennett, Mabel Normand

9 *The Fatal High C* 1r
Directed by Sennett

11 *The Passing of Izzy* 1r
Directed by Nichols
Charles Murray

13 *A Bath House Beauty* 1r
Directed by Arbuckle

18 *Mabel at the Wheel* 2r
Directed by Normand
Charles Chaplin, Mabel Normand, Harry McCoy, Chester Conklin, Mack Sennett
[Reissued as *His Daredevil Queen* by W. H. Productions]

20 *Twenty Minutes of Love* 2r
Directed by Madden
Charles Chaplin, Minta Durfee, Chester Conklin, Edgar Kennedy

23 *Where Hazel Met the Villain* 1r Directed by Arbuckle

25 *Bowery Boys* 1r Directed by Nichols

27 *Caught in a Cabaret* 2r
Directed by Normand
Charles Chaplin, Mabel Normand, Alice Davenport, Harry McCoy, Chester Conklin, Mack Swain, Minta Durfee, Alice Howell, Edgar Kennedy,

Hank Mann, Gordon Griffith,
Phyllis Allen
[Reissued as *The Jazz Waiter*
by W. H. Productions]

30 *When Villains Wait* 1r
Directed by Nichols

MAY

4 *Caught in the Rain* 1r
Directed by Chaplin
Charles Chaplin, Mack Swain,
Alice Davenport

7 *The Morning Papers* ½r
Directed by Madden
[An educational short subject]
*A Busy Day* ½r Directed
by Sennett
Charles Chaplin, Mack Swain

9 *A Suspended Ordeal* 1r
Directed by Arbuckle
Roscoe Arbuckle

11 *Finnegan's Bomb* 1r
Directed by Nichols

14 *Down on the Farm* 1r
Directed by Madden

16 *Mabel's Nerve* 1r
Mabel Normand

18 *The Water Dog* 1r
Roscoe Arbuckle

21 *When Reuben Fooled the
Bandits* 1r

23 *Acres of Alfalfa* ½r
[An educational short subject]
*Our Large Birds* ½r
[An educational short subject]

25 *A Fatal Flirtation* 1r
Charles Murray

28 *The Alarm* 2r Directed by
Arbuckle
Roscoe Arbuckle, Mabel Normand

JUNE

1 *The Fatal Mallet* 1r
Directed by Chaplin
Charles Chaplin, Mack Sennett, Mack Swain, Mabel Normand

4 *Her Friend the Bandit* 1r
Directed by Chaplin
Charles Chaplin, Charles
Murray, Mabel Normand

6 *Our Country Cousin* 1r

11 *The Knock-out* 2r
Charles Chaplin, Roscoe Arbuckle, Minta Durfee, Al St.
John, Edgar Kennedy, Mack
Swain, Hank Mann, Alice
Howell, Slim Summerville,
Charles Chase, Mack Sennett
[Reissued as *The Pugilist* by
W. H. Productions]

13 *Mabel's Busy Day* 1r
Directed by Chaplin and Normand
Charles Chaplin, Mabel Normand, Harry McCoy, Chester
Conklin, Slim Summerville

15 *A Gambling Rube* 1r

18 *A Missing Bride* 1r

20 *Mabel's Married Life* 1r
Directed by Chaplin and Normand
Charles Chaplin, Mabel Nor-

mand, Harry McCoy, Hank Mann, Mack Swain, Wallace MacDonald, Alice Howell [Reissued as *The Squarehead* by W. H. Productions]

22 *An Eavesdropper*  1r

25 *Fatty and the Heiress*  1r
Directed by Arbuckle
Roscoe Arbuckle

29 *Caught in Tights*  1r

JULY

2 *Fatty's Finish*  1r
Directed by Arbuckle
Roscoe Arbuckle

4 *Love and Bullets*  1r
Charles Murray
[Reissued as *The Trouble Mender* by W. H. Productions]

6 *A Rowboat Romance*  1r

9 *Laughing Gas*  1r
Directed by Chaplin
Charles Chaplin, Alice Howell, Slim Summerville, Mack Swain, Joseph Swickard, Fritz Schade

11 *Love and Salt Water*  ½r
*The World's Oldest Living Thing*  ½r
[An educational short subject]

16 *Mabel's New Job*  2r
Mabel Normand, Chester Conklin, Alice Davenport, Charles Chase

18 *The Sky Pirate*  1r
Roscoe Arbuckle

20 *A Fatal Sweet Tooth*  1r

23 *Those Happy Days*  1r
Directed by Arbuckle
Roscoe Arbuckle

25 *The Great Toe Mystery*  1r

27 *Soldiers of Misfortune*  1r
Charles Murray

AUGUST

1 *The Property Man*  2r
Directed by Chaplin
Charles Chaplin, Fritz Schade, Phyllis Allen, Mack Sennett
[Reissued as *The Roustabout* by W. H. Productions]

6 *A New York Girl*  2r
Mack Sennett

8 *A Coat's Tale*  1r

10 *The Face on the Barroom Floor*  1r  Directed by Chaplin
Charles Chaplin, Cecile Arnold, Fritz Schade, Chester Conklin
[Reissued as *The Ham Artist* by W. H. Productions]

13 *Recreation*  ½r  Directed by Chaplin
Charles Chaplin
*The Yosemite*  ½r
[An educational short subject]

15 *Such a Cook*  1r
Charles Murray
[Reissued as *The Bungling Burglars* by W. H. Productions]

17 *That Minstrel Man*  1r
Ford Sterling, Roscoe Arbuckle

20 *Those Country Kids* 1r
Roscoe Arbuckle, Mabel Normand
22 *Caught in a Flue* 1r
24 *Fatty's Gift* 1r Directed
by Arbuckle
Roscoe Arbuckle
27 *The Masquerader* 1r
Directed by Chaplin
Charles Chaplin, Roscoe Arbuckle, Charles Chase, Harry McCoy, Minta Durfee, Cecile Arnold, Charles Murray, Fritz Schade
29 *Her Last Chance* 1r
31 *His New Profession* 1r
Directed by Chaplin
Charles Chaplin, Charles Chase
[Reissued as *The Good-for-Nothing* by W. H. Productions]

SEPTEMBER

3 *The Baggage Smasher* 1r
5 *A Brand New Hero* 1r
Roscoe Arbuckle
7 *The Rounders* 1r Directed
by Chaplin
Charles Chaplin, Roscoe Arbuckle, Minta Durfee, Phyllis Allen, Al St. John, Charles Chase, Fritz Schade
10 *Mabel's Latest Prank* 1r
Mabel Normand
[Reissued as *A Touch of Rheumatism* by W. H. Productions]
12 *Mabel's Blunder* 1r

Mabel Normand
14 *All at Sea* 1r
17 *Bombs and Bangs* 1r
19 *Lover's Luck* 1r
21 *He Loved the Ladies* 1r
24 *The New Janitor* 1r
Directed by Chaplin
Charles Chaplin, Al St. John, Jack Dillon
[Reissued as *The New Porter* by W. H. Productions]
26 *Fatty's Debut* 1r Directed
by Arbuckle
Roscoe Arbuckle
[Reissued as *Fatty Butts In* by W. H. Productions]
28 *Hard Cider* 1r
Rube Miller

OCTOBER

1 *Killing Horace* 1r
3 *Fatty Again* 1r Directed
by Arbuckle
Roscoe Arbuckle
[Reissued as *Fatty the Four-flusher* by W. H. Productions]
5 *Their Ups and Downs* 1r
Roscoe Arbuckle
8 *Hello Mabel* 1r
Mabel Normand
10 *Those Love Pangs* 1r
Directed by Chaplin
Charles Chaplin, Chester Conklin, Cecil Arnold
12 *The Anglers* 1r
Charles Murray
15 *High Spots on Broadway* 1r
Rube Miller
[Reissued as *Having a Good Time* by W. H. Productions]

184

17 *Zip, the Dodger* 1r
Roscoe Arbuckle

19 *Dash, Love and Splash* ½r
*Santa Catalina Island and Her
Marine Gardens* ½r
[An educational short subject]

22 *The Love Thief* 1r
Chester Conklin

24 *Stout Heart but Weak Knees*
1r
Charles Murray

26 *Shot in the Excitement* 1r
Alice Howell
*Dough and Dynamite* 2r
Directed by Chaplin
Charles Chaplin, Chester
Conklin, Fritz Schade, Norma
Nichols, Vivian Edwards,
Cecil Arnold, Phyllis Allen,
Charles Chase
[Reissued as *The Doughnut
Designers* by W. H. Productions]

29 *Gentlemen of Nerve* 1r
Directed by Chaplin
Charles Chaplin, Mabel Normand, Chester Conklin, Mack
Swain, Phyllis Allen, Slim
Summerville, Charles Chase
[Reissued as *Some Nerve* by
W. H. Productions]

31 *Cursed by His Beauty* 1r
Charles Murray, Charles
Chase, Slim Summerville

NOVEMBER

2 *Lovers Post Office* 1r

Roscoe Arbuckle, Mabel Normand

5 *Curses! They Remarked* 1r
Chester Conklin

7 *His Musical Career* 1r
Directed by Chaplin
Charles Chaplin, Mack Swain,
Alice Howell

9 *His Talented Wife* 1r
Mack Sennett, Charles Murray
*His Trysting Place* 2r
Directed by Chaplin
Charles Chaplin, Mabel Normand, Mack Swain, Phyllis
Allen

12 *An Incompetent Hero* 1r
Roscoe Arbuckle

14 *How Heroes Are Made* 1r
Emma Clifton, Chester
Conklin

16 *Fatty's Jonah Day* 1r
Roscoe Arbuckle, Mabel Normand, Phyllis Allen

19 *The Noise of Bombs* 1r
Charles Murray, Edgar Kennedy

21 *Fatty's Wine Party* 1r
Roscoe Arbuckle, Mabel Normand, Syd Chaplin (his first
Keystone role)

23 *The Sea Nymphs* 2r
Roscoe Arbuckle, Mabel Normand, Mack Swain
[Reissued as *His Diving
Beauty* by W. H. Productions]
*His Taking Ways* 1r
Chester Conklin

26 *His Halted Career* 1r
Charles Murray

28 *Among the Mourners* 1r

30 *Leading Lizzie Astray* 1r
Minta Durfee, Roscoe Arbuckle, Mack Swain

DECEMBER

3 *Shotguns That Kick* 1r
Roscoe Arbuckle

5 *Getting Acquainted* 1r
Directed by Chaplin
Charles Chaplin, Phyllis Allen, Mabel Normand, Mack Swain, Cecile Arnold, Harry McCoy, Edgar Kennedy

7 *Other People's Business* 1r
*His Prehistoric Past* 2r
Directed by Chaplin
Charles Chaplin, Mack Swain, Fritz Schade, Gene Marsh
[Reissued as *The Hula Hula Dance* by W. H. Productions]

10 *The Plumber* 1r
Charles Murray, Joseph Swickard

12 *Ambrose's First Falsehood* 1r
Mack Swain, Minta Durfee

[Reissued as *In Loving Memory* by W. H. Productions]

14 *Tillie's Punctured Romance* 6r Directed by Sennett
Marie Dressler, Charles Chaplin, Mabel Normand, Mack Swain, Charles Bennett, and the rest of the Keystone comedians in lesser roles
*Fatty's Magic Pants* 1r
Roscoe Arbuckle, Bert Roach
[Reissued as *Fatty's Suitless Day* by W. H. Productions]

17 *Hogan's Annual Spree* 1r
Charles Murray

19 *A Colored Girl's Love* 1r

21 *Wild West Love* 1r
Chester Conklin
*Fatty and Minnie-He-Haw* 2r
Roscoe Arbuckle, Minta Durfee, Princess Minnie

24 *Their Fatal Bumping* 1r

26 *His Second Childhood* 1r
Charles Murray

28 *Gussle, the Golfer* 1r
Syd Chaplin, Mack Swain, Dixie Chene

31 *A Dark Lover's Play* 1r

## *1915*

JANUARY

2 *Hogan's Wild Oats* ½r
Directed by Avery
Charles Murray
*A Steel Rolling Mill* ½r
[An educational short subject]

4 *Hushing the Scandal* 2r

Chester Conklin, Syd Chaplin
[Reissued as *Friendly Enemies* by W. H. Productions]
*Her Winning Punch* ½r
Slim Summerville
*The United States Army in San Francisco* ½r

[An educational short subject]

7 *Giddy, Gay and Ticklish* 1r
Syd Chaplin, Phyllis Allen
[Reissued as *A Gay Lothario*
by W. H. Productions]

9 *Only A Farmer's Daughter*
1r
Charles Chase, Vivian Edwards, Fritz Schade

11 *Rum and Wall Paper* 1r

14 *Mabel and Fatty's Wash Day*
1r
Mabel Normand, Roscoe Arbuckle

16 *Hash House Mashers* 1r
Charles Chase, Fritz Schade,
Frank Opperman, Virginia
Chester, Chester Conklin

18 *Mabel and Fatty's Simple Life*
2r
Mabel Normand, Roscoe Arbuckle
*Love, Speed and Thrills* 1r
Mack Swain, Chester Conklin, Minta Durfee

21 *Hogan's Mussy Job* 1r
Directed by Avery
Charles Murray

23 *Fatty and Mabel at the San
Diego Exposition* 1r
Roscoe Arbuckle, Mabel Normand

25 *Colored Villainy* 1r

28 *Mabel, Fatty and the Law*
1r
Mabel Normand, Roscoe Arbuckle, Harry Gribbon, Frank
Hayes, Minta Durfee

[Reissued as *Fatty's Spooning
Day* by W. H. Productions]

30 *Peanuts and Bullets* 1r
Directed by Cogley
Nick Cogley

FEBRUARY

1 *The Home Breakers* 2r
Mack Swain, Chester Conklin,
Alice Davenport, Minta Durfee, Slim Summerville
[Reissued as *Other People's
Wives* by Harry Aitken]
*Fatty's New Role* 1r
Roscoe Arbuckle

4 *Hogan the Porter* 1r
Directed by Avery
Charles Murray

6 *Caught in a Park* 1r

8 *A Bird's a Bird* 1r
Chester Conklin

11 *Fatty and Mabel's Married
Life* 1r
Roscoe Arbuckle, Mabel Normand

13 *Hogan's Romance Upset* 1r
Directed by Avery
Charles Murray

15 *Hogan's Aristocratic Dream*
2r Directed by Avery
Charles Murray, Bobby Dunn

18 *Ye Olden Grafter* ½r
Mack Swain, Harry Gribbon
*A Glimpse of the San Diego
Exposition* ½r
[An educational short subject]

20 *Hearts and Planets* 1r

187

Chester Conklin, Mack Sennett, Minta Durfee

22 *A Lucky Leap* 1r
Nick Cogley

25 *That Springtime Feeling* 1r
Syd Chaplin

27 *Hogan Out West* 1r
Directed by Avery
Charles Murray

MARCH

1 *Ambrose's Sour Grapes* 2r
Mack Swain, Chester Conklin,
Harry Gribbon
*Wilful Ambrose* 1r
Mack Swain, Louise Fazenda

4 *Fatty's Reckless Fling* 1r
Roscoe Arbuckle

6 *From Patches to Plenty* 1r
Charles Murray, Ethel Madison, Mack Swain, Vivian Edwards

8 *Fatty's Chance Acquaintance*
1r
Roscoe Arbuckle

11 *Love in Armor* 1r
Roscoe Arbuckle, Max Davidson, Charles Chase

13 *Beating Hearts and Carpets*
1r

15 *That Little Band of Gold* 2r
Roscoe Arbuckle, Mabel Nor-
mand, Ford Sterling, Ethel
Madison
[Reissued as *For Better or
Worse* by W. H. Productions]
*Ambrose's Little Hatchet* 1r
Mack Swain, Louise Fazenda,
Don Barclay

20 *Fatty's Faithful Fido* 1r
Roscoe Arbuckle

22 *A One Night Stand* 1r
Directed by Harry McCoy
Chester Conklin, Mae Busch,
William Engle, Harry McCoy,
Vivian Edwards, Frank Bond,
Eunice Hughes

25 *Ambrose's Fury* 1r
Directed by Dell Henderson
Mack Swain, Louise Fazenda,
Alice Davenport

27 *Caught in the Act* 1r

29 *Gussle's Day of Rest* 2r
Directed by Avery
Syd Chaplin, Cecil Arnold,
Slim Summerville
*Settled at the Seaside* ½r
Charles Chase, Mae Busch
*Viewing Sherman Institute
for Indians at Riverside,
California* ½r
[An educational short sub-
ject]

APRIL

1 *When Love Took Wings* 1r
Roscoe Arbuckle

3 *Ambrose's Lofty Perch* 1r
Directed by Dell Henderson
Mack Swain, Louise Fazenda,
Don Barclay

5 *Droppington's Devilish
Dream* 1r
Chester Conklin

8 *The Rent Jumpers* 1r
Directed by Frank Griffin
Mae Busch, Fritz Schade,

188

Frank Opperman, Charles
Chase
10 *Gussle's Wayward Path* 1r
Directed by Avery
Syd Chaplin, Phyllis Allen
12 *Droppington's Family Tree*
2r
Chester Conklin
*The Beauty Bunglers* 1r
Charles Murray
15 *Do-Re-Me-Fa* 1r
Chester Conklin
17 *Ambrose's Nasty Temper* 1r
Mack Swain
19 *His Luckless Love* 1r
*Wished on Mabel* 1r
Mabel Normand
22 *Mabel and Fatty Viewing the
World's Fair at San Francisco*
1r
Mabel Normand, Roscoe Ar-
buckle
24 *Love, Loot and Crash* 1r
Charles Chase, Dora Rogers,
Joseph Swickard, Fritz Schade
26 *Their Social Splash* 1r
Directed by Arvid Gillstrom
Charles Murray, Polly Moran,
Mabel Normand, Slim Sum-
merville
*Gussle Rivals Jonah* 2r
Directed by Avery
Syd Chaplin
29 *A Bear Affair* 1r
Louise Fazenda, Harry
McCoy

**MAY**

1 *Mabel's Wilful Way* 1r
Mabel Normand

3 *Gussle's Backward Way* 1r
Directed by Avery
Syd Chaplin
6 *Gussle Tied to Trouble* 1r
Directed by Avery
Syd Chaplin
8 *A Human Hound's Triumph*
1r
Mack Swain, Harry McCoy,
Fritz Schade
10 *Our Daredevil Chief* 2r
Ford Sterling, Mack Swain,
Minta Durfee, Al St. John,
Harry Bernard
13 *Crossed Love and Swords*
1r Directed by Frank Griffin
Louise Fazenda, Dave Morris,
Harry Bernard, Al St. John
15 *Miss Fatty's Seaside Lovers*
1r
Roscoe Arbuckle
22 *For Better–But Worse* 1r
Harry McCoy
29 *A Versatile Villain* 1r
Directed by Frank Griffin
Charles Chase, Louise
Fazenda
30 *He Wouldn't Stay Down* 1r
Ford Sterling
31 *Those College Girls* 2r
Charles Murray, Polly Moran,
Slim Summerville
[Reissued as *His Bitter Half*
by W. H. Productions]

**JUNE**

3 *Mabel Lost and Won* 1r
Mabel Normand, Owen
Moore, Mack Swain

189

7 *Those Bitter Sweets* 1r
Harry McCoy

10 *A Hash House Fraud* 1r
Louise Fazenda, Chester
Conklin, Fritz Schade

12 *Merely a Married Man* 1r
Harry McCoy

14 *The Cannon Ball* 2r
Chester Conklin
[Reissued by Tri-Stone Pictures and, as *The Dynamiter*,
by W. H. Productions]
*A Home Breaking Hound* 1r
Don Barclay, Dorothy Hagart,
Joseph Swickard

21 *The Little Teacher* 2r
Mabel Normand, Mack Sennett, Roscoe Arbuckle, Owen
Moore
[Reissued as *A Small Town
Bully* by W. H. Productions]

28 *Fatty's Plucky Pup* 2r
Roscoe Arbuckle

JULY

5 *Court House Crooks* 2r
Ford Sterling, Minta Durfee,
Charles Arling

12 *When Ambrose Dared Walrus*
2r

Mack Swain, Chester Conklin, Vivian Edwards

19 *Dirty Work in a Laundry* 2r
Ford Sterling, Minta Durfee,
Harry Bernard, Al St. John
[Reissued as *A Desperate
Scoundrel* by W. H. Productions]

26 *Fatty's Tin Type Tangle* 2r
Roscoe Arbuckle, Louise
Fazenda, Edgar Kennedy

AUGUST

2 *A Lover's Lost Control* 2r
Directed by Avery
Syd Chaplin
[Reissued as *Looking Them
Over* by W. H. Productions]

9 *A Rascal of Wolfish Ways* 2r
Mae Busch, Charles Arling,
Fritz Schade
[Reissued as *A Polished Villain* by W. H. Productions]

16 *The Battle of Ambrose and
Walrus* 2r
Mack Swain, Chester Conklin, Dora Rodgers, Harry Bernard

23 *Only a Messenger Boy* 2r
Ford Sterling

## TRIANGLE-KEYSTONE COMEDIES
(2r unless otherwise noted)

### *1915*

OCTOBER

27 *My Valet* 4r Directed by
Mack Sennett
Raymond Hitchcock, Mack
Sennett, Mabel Normand,

Frank Opperman, Alice Davenport, Fred Mace

NOVEMBER

7 *A Game Old Knight*

Directed by Richard Jones
Charles Murray, Louise
Fazenda, Harry Booker, Slim
Summerville, Cecile Arnold,
Edgar Kennedy

14 *A Favorite Fool*   Directed by
Dell Henderson and E. A.
Frazee
Eddie Foy, Polly Moran,
Charles Arling, Mae Busch,
the Seven Little Foys

*Fickle Fatty's Fall*   Directed
by Roscoe Arbuckle
Roscoe Arbuckle, Ivy Crosth-
waite, Alice Davenport, Bob-
by Vernon, May Emory, Guy
Woodward, Minta Durfee,
Phyllis Allen, Al St. John,
Glen Cavender

21 *Her Painted Hero*   Directed
by Richard Jones
Hale Hamilton, Charles Murray, Slim Summerville, Polly
Moran, Harry Booker

*Saved by Wireless*   Directed
by Walter Wright
Mack Swain, Chester Conklin,
Ora Carew, Harry McCoy,
Andy Anderson, Nick Cogley
Walter Klintberg

28 *Stolen Magic*   Directed by
Mack Sennett
Mack Sennett, Raymond
Hitchcock, Mabel Normand,
Alice Davenport, Frank Hayes

*His Father's Footsteps*
Directed by Ford Sterling
Ford Sterling, Charles Chase

DECEMBER

5 *A Janitor's Wife's Temptation*
Directed by Dell Henderson
Fred Mace, Martha Golden,
Harry Gribbon, Jay Lewis,
Betty Marsh

*The Best of Enemies*
Directed by Frank Griffin
Joe Weber, Lew Fields, Mae
Busch, Joseph Swickard,
Billie Bennett, Chester Conk-
lin, Mack Swain, Guy Wood-
ward, Frank Opperman

12 *The Village Scandal*
Directed by Roscoe Arbuckle
Roscoe Arbuckle, Raymond
Hitchcock, Flora Zabelle, Al
St. John, Harry McCoy

*The Great Vacuum Robbery*
Directed by Richard Jones
Charles Murray, Louise Fa-
zenda, Slim Summerville, Ed-
gar Kennedy, Harry Booker,
Dixie Chene, Wayland Trask

19 *Crooked to the End*
Directed by E. A. Frazee and
Walter Reed
Fred Mace, Anna Luther,
Charles Arling, Hugh Fay,
Earl Rodney

*Fatty and the Broadway Stars*
Directed by Roscoe Arbuckle
Roscoe Arbuckle, Ivy Crosth-
waite, Joe Weber, Lew Fields,
Sam Bernard, Al St. John,
William Collier, Sr., Joe Jack-
son, Ford Sterling, Mack
Sennett

26 *A Submarine Pirate* 4r
Directed by Charles Avery
and Syd Chaplin
Syd Chaplin, Glen Cavender,
Wesley Ruggles, Phyllis Allen
*The Hunt* Directed by Ford
Sterling and Charles Chase
Ford Sterling, Polly Moran,
May Emory, Bobby Vernon,
Fritz Schade, Guy Woodward,
Frank Opperman, Dorothy
Hagart

## 1916

JANUARY

2 *Dizzy Heights and Daring
Hearts* Directed by Walter
Wright
Chester Conklin, Dave Anderson, Cora Anderson, William
Mason, Nick Cogley
*The Worst of Friends*
Directed by Frank Griffin
Joe Weber, Lew Fields, Alice
Davenport, Mae Busch, Harry
Gribbon

9 *The Great Pearl Tangle*
Directed by Dell Henderson
Sam Bernard, Harry Gribbon,
Harry McCoy, Minta Durfee,
Mildred Adams
*Fatty and Mabel Adrift* 3r
Directed by Roscoe Arbuckle
Roscoe Arbuckle, Mabel Normand, Al St. John, Frank
Hayes, May Wells, Wayland
Trask, Glen Cavender, James
Bryant, Joe Bordeau

16 *A Modern Enoch Arden*
Directed by Clarence Badger
Joe Jackson, Mack Swain,
Hank Mann, Dora Rogers,
Betty Marsh, Vivian Edwards
*Because He Loved Her*

Directed by Dell Henderson
Sam Bernard, Glen Cavender,
Mae Busch, Harry McCoy

23 *A Movie Star* Directed by
Fred Fishback
Mack Swain, Louella Maxam,
May Wells, Ray Grey, Phyllis
Allen, Harry McCoy
*Perils of the Park* Directed
by Dell Henderson
Harry Gribbon, Alice Davenport, Marie Manley, Harry
McCoy

30 *Love Will Conquer*
Directed by E. A. Frazee
Mack Swain, Fred Mace,
Harry Gribbon, Polly Moran,
Joseph Swickard, Billie
Brockwell, Harry McCoy
*He Did and He Didn't*
Directed by Roscoe Arbuckle
Roscoe Arbuckle, Mabel Normand, William Jefferson, Al
St. John
[Sometimes referred to by its
working title, *Love and Lobsters*]

FEBRUARY

6 *His Hereafter* Directed by
Richard Jones

192

Charles Murray, Louise Fazenda, Harry Booker, Pat Kelley, Myrtle Lind, Edgar Kennedy, Wayland Trask [Sometimes referred to by its working title, *Murray's Mixup*]

*His Pride and Shame*
Directed by Ford Sterling and Charles Chase
Ford Sterling, Juanita Hansen, Bobby Vernon, Bobby Dunn, Guy Woodward

13 *Better Late Than Never*
Directed by Frank Griffin and Jean Havez
William Collier, Sr., Mae Busch, Frank Opperman, Joseph Belmont
[Sometimes referred to by its working title, *Getting Married*]

*Fido's Fate*   Directed by Frank Griffin
Charles Murray, Alice Davenport, Fritz Schade, May Emory, Frank Hayes

20 *The Bright Lights*   Directed by Roscoe Arbuckle
Roscoe Arbuckle, Mabel Normand, James Bryant, Minta Durfee, G. A. Ely
[Sometimes referred to by its working title, *The Lure of Broadway*]

*His Auto Ruination*
Directed by Fred Fishback
Mack Swain, Harry Gribbon,

Julia Faye, May Wells, Harry McCoy, Bobby Dunn

27 *Cinders of Love*   Directed by Walter Wright
Chester Conklin, Slim Summerville, Claire Anderson, Billie Bennett, Lois Holmes, William Mason, Harry McCoy

MARCH

5 *Wife and Auto Trouble*
Directed by Dell Henderson
William Collier, Sr., Mae Busch, Blanche Payson, Joseph Belmont, Alice Davenport

*The Judge*
Charles Murray, Louise Fazenda, Harry Booker, Wayland Trask, Phyllis Allen

12 *The Village Blacksmith*
Directed by Hank Mann
Hank Mann, Vivian Edwards, Glen Cavender, Reece Gardiner, Tom Kennedy, Polly Moran

*The Village Vampire*
Directed by E. A. Frazee
Fred Mace, Anna Luther, Joseph Swickard, Earl Rodney, Billie Brockwell, Dale Fuller, Max Davidson
[Sometimes referred to by its working title, *The Great Leap*]

19 *Gypsy Joe*   Directed by Clarence Badger and William Campbell

Joe Jackson, Marion de la Parelle, Dora Rogers, Jack "Shorty" Hamilton, Louis Morrison, Elizabeth De Witt, Betty Marsh

*A Love Riot*   Directed by Richard Jones

Charles Murray, Louise Fazenda, Harry Booker, Alice Davenport, Dora Rogers, Wayland Trask

26 *By Stork Delivery*
Directed by Fred Fishback
Mack Swain, Polly Moran, May Emory, Vin Moore, Baby Marie Kiernan, Joe Lee, Ivy Crosthwaite, Bobby Dunn

*An Oily Scoundrel*
Directed by E. A. Frazee
Fred Mace, Dale Fuller, Louella Maxam, Earl Rodney, Charles Arling, Hugh Fay

APRIL

2 *His Wife's Mistakes*
Directed by Roscoe Arbuckle
Roscoe Arbuckle, Al St. John, Minta Durfee, Betty Gray, William Jefferson, Arthur Earl

*A Bath House Blunder*
Directed by Dell Henderson
Joe Jackson, Mae Busch, Joseph Belmont, Frank Hayes, Polly Moran, Blanche Payson, Don Likes

9 *His Bread and Butter*
Directed by Eddie Cline and Hank Mann

Hank Mann, Peggy Pearce, Slim Summerville, Bobby Dunn

*His Last Laugh*   Directed by Walter Wright

Harry McCoy, Julia Faye, Mary Thurman, Joseph Callahan, Billie Bennett, Sutherland Ring, Dave Anderson, Lige Crommie

16 *The Other Man*   Directed by Roscoe Arbuckle
Roscoe Arbuckle, Irene Wallace, Horace J. Haines, Lillian Shaffner, Al St. John, Minta Durfee, William Jefferson, Joe Bordeau

*Bucking Society*   Directed by Harry Williams and William Campbell
Chester Conklin, Jack "Shorty" Hamilton, Louella Maxam, Dora Rogers, Jack Henderson

23 *The Snow Cure*   Directed by Arvid Gillstrom
Ford Sterling, Fritz Schade, Marie Manley, Alice Davenport, James Donnelly

*A Rough Knight*   A Shorty Hamilton Kay Bee Comedy
[This was the first of many Triangle comedies which filled in the release schedule but were not produced by Sennett. Triangle had established a comedy company at the Fine Arts Studio which produced shorts featuring De Wolfe

194

Hopper, Shorty Hamilton, and Fay Tincher. Many Keystone supporting players appeared in these comedies which were mainly directed by Eddie Dillon. Since many works on Keystone have included these films as a part of Sennett's output, they are included here and specifically differentiated for the reader.]

30 *The Lion and the Girl*
Directed by Glen Cavender
Joe Jackson, Claire Anderson, May Wells, Louis Morrison, Clarence Lyndon, Billy Hauber, Leo Kendal
*His Bitter Pill*
Directed by Fred Fishback
Mack Swain, Louella Maxam, Ella Haines, Edgar Kennedy

MAY

7 *A Dash of Courage*
Directed by Charles Chase
Harry Gribbon, Wallace Beery, Guy Woodward, Gloria Swanson, William Mason, Bobby Vernon, Frank Opperman
*Her Marble Heart*
Directed by Richard Jones
Charles Murray, Louise Fazenda, Harry Booker, Frank Hayes, Wayland Trask

14 *Bath Tub Perils* Directed by E. A. Frazee
Fred Mace, Claire Anderson, Dale Fuller, Hugh Fay

*The Moonshiners*
Directed by Roscoe Arbuckle
Al St. John, Alice Lake, Joe Bordeau, Horace J. Haines

28 *Bubbles of Trouble*
Directed by Eddie Cline
Harry McCoy, Peggy Pearce, Bobby Dunn, Jack Henderson, Billy Gilbert, James Donnelly
*The Two O'Clock Train*
A Fay Tincher Triangle Comedy

JUNE

4 *Hearts and Sparks*
Directed by Charles Chase
Hank Mann, Bobby Vernon, Gloria Swanson, Nick Cogley, Billie Bennett, Tom Kennedy

11 *The Mystery of the Leaping Fish* A Douglas Fairbanks-Bessie Love Triangle Comedy

18 *His First False Step*
Directed by William Campbell
Chester Conklin, Mary Thurman, May Wells, Charles Reisner, Dora Rogers, Lee Morris
*Bedelia's Bluff* A Fay Tincher Triangle Comedy

25 *The Waiter's Ball* Directed by Roscoe Arbuckle and Ferris Hartman
Roscoe Arbuckle, Al St. John, Corinne Parquet, Kate Price, Joe Bordeau, Alice Lake
*His Wild Oats* Directed by

Ford Sterling and Clarence Badger
Ford Sterling, Mack Swain, Polly Moran, Vivian Edwards, Guy Woodward, Ella Haines, Harry Gribbon, Joseph Swickard

2 *Wings and Wheels*
Directed by Walter Wright
Ora Carew, Joseph Belmont
*Poor Papa* A De Wolfe Hopper Triangle Comedy

9 *The Surf Girl* Directed by Harry Edwards
Glen Cavender, Raymond Griffith, Dale Fuller, Albert T. Gillespie, Fritz Schade
*Laundry Liz* A Fay Tincher Triangle Comedy

16 *Madcap Ambrose* Directed by Fred Fishback
Mack Swain, Polly Moran, May Wells, Edgar Kennedy, Frank Hayes, May Emory, Louis Morrison
*A Social Cub* Directed by Clarence Badger
Bobby Vernon, Gloria Swanson, Reggie Morris

25 *Pills of Peril* Directed by Richard Jones
Charles Murray, Louise Fazenda, Wayland Trask, Alice Davenport, Myrtle Lind, Harry Booker
*Never Again* A William Collier, Sr., Triangle Comedy

30 *A La Cabaret* Directed by Walter Wright
Ora Carew, Joseph Belmont, Blanche Payson, Joseph Callahan, Nick Cogley, Mal St. Clair
*Skirts* A Fay Tincher Triangle Comedy

6 *The Feathered Nest*
Directed by Frank Griffin and Edward Chandler
Charles Murray, Louise Fazenda, Harry Booker, Wayland Trask
[Sometimes referred to by its working title, *Girl Guardian*, and reissued by Triangle in 1920 as *Only a Farmer's Daughter*]
*The Girl and the Mummy*
A De Wolfe Hopper Triangle Comedy

13 *The Danger Girl*
Directed by Clarence Badger
Bobby Vernon, Gloria Swanson, Helen Bray, Myrtle Lind
[Sometimes referred to by its working title, *Love on Skates*]
*Puppets* A De Wolfe Hopper Triangle Comedy

20 *The Winning Punch*
Directed by Eddie Cline
Slim Summerville, Peggy Pearce, Bob Finlay, Bobby Dunn
*His Lying Heart* Directed by

196

Ford Sterling and Charles Avery
Ford Sterling, Vivian Edwards, Louella Maxam, Paul Jacobs, Charles Reisner

27 *Vampire Ambrose* Directed by Fred Fishback
Mack Swain, May Emory, Polly Moran
*The French Milliner* A Fay Tincher Triangle Comedy

SEPTEMBER

3 *Maid Mad* Directed by Frank Griffin
Charles Murray, Louise Fazenda, Wayland Trask, Harry Booker
[Sometimes referred to by its working title, *The Fortune Teller*]
*A Lover's Might* Directed by Harry Edwards
Fred Mace, Harry Gribbon, Louis Morrison, Julia Faye, Billy Armstrong
[Sometimes referred to by its working title, *The Fire Chief*]

10 *She Loved a Sailor*
Directed by Victor Heerman
Claire Anderson, Hugh Fay, Jack "Shorty" Hamilton, Harry McCoy
*Dollars and Sense*
Directed by Walter Wright and Andy Anderson
Ora Carew, Joseph Belmont, Mal St. Clair, Blanche Payson, Nick Cogley, Lige Crom-

mie, Joseph Callahan
[Sometimes referred to by its working title, *The Twins*]

OCTOBER

1 *Haystacks and Steeples*
Directed by Clarence Badger and Bert Lund
Gloria Swanson, Reggie Morris, Della Pringle, George Felix, Eva Thatcher, Helen Bray, Joseph Swickard
*The Lady Drummer* A Fay Tincher Triangle Comedy

8 *A Tugboat Romeo*
Directed by William Campbell and Harry Williams
Chester Conklin, Guy Woodward, Marie Manley, Martha Trick
*Bombs* Directed by Frank Griffin
Charles Murray, Louise Fazenda, Mary Thurman, Harry Booker, Wayland Trask, Edgar Kennedy

NOVEMBER

9 *His Busted Trust* Directed by Eddie Cline
Slim Summerville, Bobby Dunn, Peggy Pearce, Jack "Shorty" Hamilton, May Wells, Vivian Edwards
*The Scoundrel's Tale*
Directed by Glen Cavender
Mary Thurman, Dale Fuller, Gene Rogers, Edgar Kennedy, Raymond Griffith

197

Release dates for the following Keystone-Triangles have been obscured by the pages of time. It is known that the Triangle release schedule continued to make use of the Triangle comedies directed by Eddie Dillon and starring Fay Tincher, Jack Cooper, and others.

*Ambrose's Cup of Woe*
Directed by Fred Fishback
and Herman Raymaker
Mack Swain, May Emory,
Paul Jacobs, Edgar Kennedy,
Joseph Swickard

*Ambrose's Rapid Rise*
Directed by Fred Fishback
Mack Swain, Louella Maxam,
Tom Kennedy, Robert Kortman

*Safety First Ambrose*
Directed by Fred Fishback
Mack Swain, May Wells,
Helen Bray, Robert Kortman,
Alice Jorgens
[Sometimes referred to by its working title, *Sheriff Ambrose*]

*A Creampuff Romance*
Directed by Roscoe Arbuckle
Roscoe Arbuckle, Alice Lake
[Sometimes referred to by its working titles, *His Alibi* and

*A Reckless Romeo*]
*Love Comet*  Directed by
Walter Wright
Ora Carew, Joseph Belmont

*The Three Slims*
Slim Summerville, Victor Potel, Mal St. Clair
[Possibly a working title for another release]

*His Last Scent*  Directed by
Charles Avery
Fred Mace, Alice Davenport,
Cecile Arnold, Fritz Schade,
Victor Potel

*No One to Guide Him*
Syd Chaplin, Phyllis Allen

*Black Eyes and Blue*
Directed by Robert Kerr and
E. G. Kenton
Billy Armstrong, Martha
Trick, Juanita Hansen, Jack
Henderson, Dot Hagart

## 1917

The exact release dates of the Keystone-Triangle comedies for the months of September, October, November, and December, 1916, along with those of January, 1917, are difficult to trace. Remember that this was the period in which Sennett had so much trouble with Triangle. The exact listing resumes below with February.

11 *The Nick of Time Baby*
Directed by Clarence Badger
Bobby Vernon, Gloria Swanson, Earl Rodney, Sylvia Ashton, Larry Lyndon, Teddy

18 *Stars and Bars*   Directed by
Victor Heerman
Ford Sterling, Harry Gribbon, Gene Rogers, May Emory, Hugh Fay

25 *Maggie's First False Step*
Directed by Frank Griffin
Charles Murray, Louise Fazenda, Harry Booker, Alice Davenport, Wallace Beery, Mary Thurman

MARCH

4 *Villa of the Movies*
Directed by Eddie Cline
Slim Summerville, Peggy Pearce, Bobby Dunn

11 *Dodging His Doom*
Directed by William Campbell and Harry Williams
Chester Conklin, Dale Fuller, Wayland Trask, Guy Woodward, Dora Rogers

18 *Her Circus Knight*
Directed by Walter Wright
Ora Carew, Joseph Belmont, Joseph Callahan, Blanche Payson, Lige Crommie, Mal St. Clair, Nick Cogley
[Sometimes referred to by its working title, *The Circus Girl*]

25 *Her Fame and Shame*
Directed by Frank Griffin

Charles Murray, Louise Fazenda, Polly Moran, Slim Summerville, Edgar Kennedy, Sylvia Ashton, Harry Booker, Frank Opperman

APRIL

1 *Pinched in the Finish*
Myrtle Lind, Ford Sterling, Harry Gribbon, Mary Thurman

8 *Her Nature Dance*
Directed by William Campbell
Marie Prevost, Eva Thatcher, Fritz Schade, Alice Lake, Gene Rogers

15 *Teddy at the Throttle*
Directed by Clarence Badger
Bobby Vernon, Gloria Swanson, Wallace Beery, Teddy

22 *Secrets of a Beauty Parlor*
Directed by Harry Williams
Earl Rodney, Marie Prevost, Alice Davenport, Bobby Dunn, Hugh Fay, Jay Dwiggens, Sylvia Ashton

29 *A Maiden's Trust*
Directed by Harry Williams
Ford Sterling, Myrtle Lind, Hugh Fay, Alice Davenport, Wayland Trask, Grover Ligon

MAY

6 *His Naughty Thought*
Directed by Fred Fishback
Mack Swain, Polly Moran, Dora Rogers, Eva Thatcher, Larry Lyndon, Robert Kortman

199

13 *Her Torpedoed Love*
Directed by Frank Griffin
Ford Sterling, Louise Fazenda, Tom Kennedy, Wayland Trask, Harry Booker

20 *A Royal Rogue*
Directed by Robert Kerr
Billy Armstrong, Raymond Griffith, Juanita Hansen, Ray Russell, Hal Cooley, Martha Trick, Jack Henderson

27 *Oriental Love* Directed by Walter Wright
Ora Carew, Joseph Belmont, Joseph Callahan, Nick Cogley, Sid Smith, Andy Anderson, Edgar Kennedy, Blanche Payson

JUNE

3 *Cactus Nell* Directed by Fred Fishback
Polly Moran, Wallace Beery, Wayland Trask, Cliff Bowes, Robert Kortman, Paul Jacobs, May Wells

10 *The Betrayal of Maggie*
Charles Murray, Louise Fazenda

17 *Skidding Hearts* Directed by Walter Wright
Ora Carew, Joseph Belmont

24 *A Dog Catcher's Love*
Directed by Eddie Cline
Slim Summerville, Glen Cavender, Peggy Pearce, Hal Cooley, Jack Henderson, Harry Breen

JULY

1 *Dangers of a Bride*
Directed by Robert Kerr and Ferris Hartman
Bobby Vernon, Gloria Swanson, Robert Milliken, Jay Dwiggens, Juanita Hansen, Al McKinnon, Martha Trick, Fritz Schade, F. B. Cooper

8 *Whose Baby?* Directed by Clarence Badger
Bobby Vernon, Gloria Swanson, Earle Rodney, Clarry Lyndon, Sylvia Ashton, Edgar Kennedy, Helen Bray

15 *A Clever Dummy* Directed by Herman Raymaker
Ben Turpin, Juanita Hansen, Chester Conklin, Wallace Beery, Claire Anderson, James Delano, James Donnelly

22 *She Needed a Doctor*
Polly Moran, Wayland Trask, James Donnelly, Eva Thatcher, Harry Booker, Fred Brown

29 *Thirst*
Mack Swain, Ethel Teare, Cliff Bowes, Larry Lyndon, May Emory, Paul Jacobs, Eva Thatcher
[Reissued under its original title by Tri-Stone Pictures in 1923]

AUGUST

5 *His Uncle Dudley*
Directed by Richard Jones and Don O'Brien

200

Polly Moran, Harry Booker, Sid Smith, Frank Hayes, Jay Dwiggens

12 *Lost—A Cook*
Mack Swain, Ben Turpin, Ethel Teare, Paul Jacobs, Mal St. Clair

19 *The Pawnbroker's Heart*
Directed by Eddie Cline
Chester Conklin, Ben Turpin, Peggy Pearce, Glen Cavender, Caroline Rankin

26 *Two Crooks* Directed by Victor Heerman
Harry Gribbon, Marie Prevost [Sometimes referred to by its working title, *A Noble Crook*]

SEPTEMBER

2 *A Shanghaied Jonah*

Billy Armstrong, Guy Woodward, Maude Wayne

9 *His Precious Life* Directed by Herman Raymaker
Slim Summerville, Charles Murray, Louise Fazenda, Dora Rogers, Wayland Trask

16 *Hula Hula Land*
Billy Armstrong, Guy Woodward, Maude Wayne, Vera Steadman

23 *The Late Lamented*
Mary Thurman, George Binns, Claire Anderson

30 *The Sultan's Wife*
Directed by Clarence Badger
Bobby Vernon, Gloria Swanson, Joseph Callahan, Phyllis Haver

# Bibliography

### 1. *Books*

Chaplin, Charles. *My Autobiography.* Simon and Schuster, 1964.

Fowler, Gene. *Father Goose.* Covici-Friede, 1934.

Griffith, Linda. *When the Movies Were Young.* N.Y., 1925.

Hall, Ben. *The Best Remaining Seats.* Clarkson-Potter, 1961.

Huff, Theodore. *Chaplin.* Abelard-Schuman, 1951.

Jacobs, Lewis. *The Rise of the American Film.* Harcourt, Brace and Company, 1939.

Lahue, Kalton C. *World of Laughter: The Motion Picture Comedy Short, 1910–1930.* University of Oklahoma Press, 1966.

Montgomery, John. *Comedy Films.* George Allen and Unwin, 1954.

Ramsaye, Terry. *A Million and One Nights.* Simon and Schuster, 1926.

Sennett, Mack. *King of Comedy.* Doubleday, 1954.

Turconi, Davide. *Mack Sennett.* Edizioni dell'Ateneo Roma, 1961.

### 2. *Periodicals*

*Exhibitor's Trade Review* (August, 1912–July, 1917).

*Los Angeles Times* (August, 1912–July, 1922).

*Motography* (August, 1912–July, 1917).
*Motion Picture News* (August, 1912–July, 1917).
*Moving Picture World* (August, 1912–July, 1917).
*Triangle News* (October, 1915–July, 1917).
*World's Work, The* (August, 1912–July, 1917).

# Index of Titles

# Index

# General Index

211

The text for *Kops and Custards* has been set on the Linotype in 11-point Times Roman, a contemporary face designed by Stanley Morison of London. Times Roman is one of our most useful body types, due to its exceptional qualities of legibility and reproduction. The paper on which the book is printed bears the watermark of the University of Oklahoma Press and has an effective life of at least three hundred years.